Revised Fourth Edition
1000 FRUIT JARS
PRICED & ILLUSTRATED
by Bill Schroeder

COLLECTOR BOOKS
A Division of Schroeder Publishing Co., Inc.

Additional copies of this book may be ordered from:

COLLECTOR BOOKS
P.O. Box 3009
Paducah, Kentucky 42001
@ $4.95 Postpaid

Copyright: Bill Schroeder, 1976
ISBN: 0-89145-011-4
Values Updated 1979

This book or any part thereof may not be reproduced without the written consent of the Publisher.

ACKNOWLEDGEMENTS

I want to thank the hundreds of fruit jar collectors, dealers and enthusiasts that were so kind in sending literally thousands of fruit jar rubbings, tracings, sketches, photos, and information. While our own jar holdings are large, it would have been impossible to compile a work such as this without their help.

We plan future editions and revisions of this price guide, and invite pencil rubbings, tracings or accurate sketches of any jar that you may have that is not included in this book. Write this information on any rubbing you send: color, sizes, type of top, lid, or closure. We will make every effort to get your jar in our next book.

We will not attempt to price jars that you have not found in this book. Please do not send tracings for us to price.

Thank you so much,

Bill Schroeder

BILL SCHROEDER

EXAMPLE

FORWARD

The 1970's will be the years of the fruit jar collector, and rightly so, for there is no other collecting field that could possibly be more interesting than assembling a group of old canning jars.

With thousands of collectors around the country searching every possible crack, crevice, attic, and cellar for these bits of history, the prices on these jars are in their infancy. The appreciation value on the rarer jars should skyrocket in the months and years ahead, with the more common issues pretty much holding their own, or advancing very slowly.

Fruit jars with unusual closures, shapes, colors and markings are much sought after by the advanced collectors, therefore command a much higher price.

If you are a beginner or novice collector, you have probably asked yourself, "Why collect fruit jars?" I ask you, "Why not?" The progress of our glass industry, manufacturing methods, the progress of our country itself is clearly revealed in the advancing cycles of the fruit jar. Nothing could be more beautiful to the collector than an old whittled wax sealer or corker, with its crude embossings and markings.

The lids, or closures, of the jars are a study within themselves as the jar manufacturers tried to improve upon the seal. These closures fall into several different classifications. The grove ring wax sealer, the tapered neck for a glass stopper or cork, threaded neck for the old zinc lid, glass lid with a wire bail, glass lid with a metal screw band. Of course, there are seveal other unique closures that never did really 'catch on', therefore they are quite rare, and command a higher market value.

For those of you who have limited space or funds to put together a larger diversified collection of several hundred jars, a collection of, say, 1858 jars would be interesting. I'm sure that there are over 50 different types of these jars, with their different sizes, colors, embossings, symbols and wording. If you didn't want to limit yourself to 1858 jars, a collection of amber jars would be nice. I know of one collection that has nothing but half pints in it. These, however, are getting quite hard to find. Pint jars might interest you, and a collection of these could still be put together at a very reasonable cost.

Other collectors are assembling series on the same type jars into sets of three to five sizes. These sets are used in the kitchen as canister sets and, I might add, they give the collector an added incentive to his already fascinating hobby. The Misson, Good Luck, Ball, Mason and Kerr series are all good examples to assemble into these different size canister sets. Most of these series have three to four sizes in them from half pint to two quart. However, I have seen sets with sizes from midgets to gallon. These are quite rare as most jar makers didn't make five or six sizes of each of their jars.

Fruit jars with chips, cracks, discoloration and other defects are virtually worthless, unless the jar is a unique or very rare item. Collectors just do not want an imperfect specimen for their collection. Manufacturing defects, pontil marks, air bubbles, whittle marks and crude imperfections made during the manufacturing process are desirable however, and in some instances command a higher price.

HOW TO BUY AND SELL FRUIT JARS

For several years now, I have been buying and selling all types of collector material. I have run ads in more than 300 different publications at considerable expense, finding that the collector magazines and papers have produced the best results for me. In these publications dealers and collectors alike are selling their material with low cost ads.

HOW TO PACK AND SHIP YOUR JARS

Extreme care must be taken when packing any glass jars for shipment. Remember these important points and you will be O.K. Separate the glass top from the jar and wrap separately. Pack each jar in a separate box before putting them into the final shipping container (a clean half-gallon milk carton works really well, using lots of newspaper). The final shipping carton should be of heavy, well constucted cardboard. Be sure to insure the package for the required amount and mark the package in heavy block letters **HANDLE WITH CARE — GLASS**.

NOTES ABOUT PRICE

The prices in this book are not an offer to buy by the publisher, but reflect a price range that dealers are asking for their jars in shops, auctions, advertisements and trade. If you were to sell your jars to a dealer you would, in most cases, get a considerably smaller amount, depending on each dealer's needs and present stock. This book does give you an idea as to the rarity of your holdings, thus the price a willing collector will pay to fill his needs. To expose your jars to the most people, you might find an ad in one of the trade publications helpful as previously mentioned under "How to Buy and Sell Fruit Jars".

There are over 1200 jars listed in this book, taking into consideration size, color and embossings. We have listed the different sizes and colors with each embossing. I am sure with each passing year different sizes, colors and embossings will turn up, making our hobby even more interesting.

OTHER BOOKS FROM COLLECTOR BOOKS

We are publishers of other fine illustrated price guides in the field of collector material, and also maintain a stock of the better books by other publishers. Send today for our illustrated leaflet that lists all the different books we stock.

Subjects covered are: Antiques, Fruit Jars, Bottles, Avon Bottles, Clocks and Watches, Straight Razors, Pocket Knives, Barbed Wire, Old Books, Coins, Stamps, United States Paper Money, Telephone Insulators, Dolls, Wicker and Oak Furniture, Cut Glass, etc.

You will like our fast service on these authoritative, up-to-date illustrated price guide books.

TRADE MARKS AND & MONOGRAMS

ANCHOR HOCKING

CONSOLIDATED F.J. CO.

BALL BROS.

BALL BROS.

LOUISVILLE GLASS CO.

J.H. FLICKINGER

HERO GLASS WKS.

HERO

GENERAL GROCERY CO.

GILCHRIST JAR CO.

ILLINOIS GLASS CO.

KERNS GORSUCH

SAFE GLASS CO.

CANTON GLASS CO.

MASON PHILA.

OLEAN GLASS CO.

PORT GLASS CO. BELLEVILLE, ILL.

ROOT GLASS CO. TERRE HAUTE, IND.

HAMILTON GLASS

HAZEL ATLAS

SALEM GLASS WKS.

TURNER GLASS CO.

WIGHTMAN

CHATTANOOGA MASON

GLENSHAW

KNOX

RUTH A GILCHRIST

HANSEE'S

ILLINOIS GLASS CO.

OWENS ILLINOIS GLASS CO.

A B G A MACHINE MADE, AQUA, 2 SIZES. GLASS LID METAL BAND. *aBga* **MASON PERFECT** MADE IN U.S.A. 12.00-15.00	**A B G A** MACHINE MADE, AQUA, 3 SIZES. GLASS LID METAL BAND. **MASON IMPROVED A B G A** 8.00-10.00	**A & CO.** HANDMADE, QUART, AQUA, GLASS LID, WIRE CLIP. *A & Co* 125.00-150.00
ACME MACHINE MADE. 3 SIZES CLEAR, SQUARE, GLASS LID WIRE BAIL. (ACME shield) 4.00-6.00	**ACME SEAL** HANDMADE, CLEAR, 3 SIZE GLASS TOP, ZINC BAND. *Acme Seal* 20.00-25.00	**ADVANCE** HANDMADE, QUART, AQUA, GLASS LID, WIRE BAIL, OR METAL CLAMP. TRADE MARK **ADVANCE** PAT. APL'D FOR 85.00-95.00
AGEE QUEEN MACHINE MADE, 4 SIZES, CLEAR, GLASS LID, TWIN TOGGLES. **AGEE QUEEN** 8.00-10.00	**AGNEW** HANDMADE, AQUA, QUART, WAX SEAL. BOTTOM READS: "JOHN AGNEW & SON" OR "AGNEW & CO." 30.00-70.00	**A G W L** HANDMADE, AQUA, QUART, WAXSEAL. AGWL PITTS PA 20.00-25.00
AIR-TIGHT HANDMADE, PINT, AMBER, ZINC LID. **AIR-TIGHT** 45.00-55.00	**ALL RIGHT** HANDMADE, QUART, AQUA, METAL DISC, WIRE CLAMP. **ALL RIGHT** 70.00-75.00	**ALL RIGHT** HANDMADE, QUART, AQUA, GLASS LID, WIRE CLAMP. **ALL RIGHT** PAT^D JAN 28TH 1868 100.00-125.00

ALMY HANDMADE, AQUA, QUART, THREADED GLASS LID. ALMY 75.00-85.00	**ALSTON** HANDMADE, AQUA, QUART, GLASS LID, WIRE BAIL. The Alston 75.00-85.00	**ALSTON** HANDMADE, CLEAR, QUART, PINT, DISC LID, WIRE CLIP, GROUND LIP.  70.00-75.00
AMAZON MACHINE MADE, CLEAR, BLUE, 3 SIZES, GLASS LID, WIRE BAIL. AMAZON SWIFT SEAL 3.00-5.00	**AMAZON SWIFT SEAL** MACHINE MADE, CLEAR, GREEN, 3 SIZES, GLASS LID, WIRE BAIL.  3.00-5.00	**AMERICAN FRUIT JAR** HANDMADE, LIGHT GREEN, QUART, GLASS LID, WIRE BAIL.  100.00-125.00
AMERICAN HANDMADE, BLUE, GREEN, 3 SIZES, ZINC LID.  18.00-22.00	**AMERICAN SODA** MACHINE MADE, CLEAR, 2 SIZES, GLASS LID, WIRE BAIL. VERTICALLY EMBOSSED "AMERICAN SODA FOUNTAIN CO." 6.00-8.00	**ANCHOR** HANDMADE, CLEAR, 3 SIZES, GLASS LID, ZINC BAND.  30.00-35.00
ANCHOR HANDMADE, CLEAR, AMBER, 3 SIZES, GLASS LID, ZINC BAND.  AMBER 20.00-25.00 OTHER 10.00-12.00	**ANCHOR HOCKING** MACHINE MADE, CLEAR, 4 SIZES, GLASS LID, WIRE BAIL.  1.00-2.00	**ANCHOR HOCKING MASON** MACHINE MADE, CLEAR, SQUARE, 3 SIZES. COMMON.  1.00-2.00

ANDERSON PRESERVING CO. MACHINE MADE, CLEAR, QUART, METAL LID. FRUIT & LEAF DESIGN AROUND JARS TOP SIDE. "ANDERSON PRESERVING CO. CAMDEN, N. J." ON BOTTOM 10.00-12.00	**A R S** HANDMADE, GROUND GLASS STOPPER. RARE. ◇A·R·S◇ STOPPER READS "A. KLINE PATD OCT. 27, 63" 100.00+	**A R S** HANDMADE, AQUA, QUART, TAPERED GLASS STOPPER. *ARS* 50.00-55.00
ARTHUR, BURNHAM & GILROY HANDMADE, AQUA, QUART WAX SEAL. ARTHUR, BURNHAM & GILROY 10th & GEO. STs PHILADELPHIA 500.00 +	**R. ARTHUR'S PATENT** HANDMADE, AQUA, QUART, WAX SEAL. R. ARTHUR'S PATENT JAN'Y 2nd 1855 250.00-275.00	**ATHERHOLT FISHER & CO.** HANDMADE, CLEAR, QUART, GROUND GLASS STOPPER. ATHERHOLT FISHER CO PHILA DA 150.00-175.00
ATLAS E-Z SEAL HANDMADE, AQUA, 3 SIZES, GLASS LID, WIRE BAIL. ATLAS E Z SEAL 8.00-10.00	**ATLAS E-Z SEAL** HANDMADE, AQUA, QUART, GLASS LID, WIRE BAIL. ATLAS E-Z SEAL 3.00-5.00	**ATLAS E-Z SEAL** MACHINE MADE, 3 SIZES GLASS LID, WIRE BAIL. "ATLAS E-Z SEAL" AMBER 20.00-25.00 OLIVE 12.00-15.00 CLEAR & GREEN 1.00
ATLAS E-Z SEAL MACHINE MADE, CLEAR, 4 SIZES, GLASS LID, WIRE BAIL. ATLAS E-Z SEAL 3.00-5.00	**ATLAS E-Z SEAL** MACHINE MADE, CLEAR, AQUA, OLIVE, 4 SIZES, GLASS LID, WIRE BAIL. "ATLAS E-Z SEAL" OLIVE 10.00-12.00 OTHER 2.00-3.00	**ATLAS** HANDMADE, AQUA, GLASS LID, WIRE BAIL. ATLAS E-Z SEAL 48-OZ 6.00-8.00

ATLAS E-Z SEAL 58-OZ	ATLAS GOOD LUCK	ATLAS GOOD LUCK
MACHINE MADE, CLEAR, 58-OZ, GLASS LID, WIRE BAIL.	MACHINE MADE, CLEAR, AQUA, 3 SIZES, GLASS LID, WIRE BAIL.	MACHINE MADE, CLEAR, HALF PINT.
"ATLAS E-Z SEAL" 58-OZ	ATLAS  GOOD LUCK	ATLAS GOOD LUCK
6.00-8.00	2.00-4.00	4.00-6.00

ATLAS	ATLAS	ATLAS
HANDMADE, AQUA, QUART, ZINC LID, RARE.	HANDMADE, AQUA, 3 SIZES, ZINC LID.	MACHINE MADE, CLEAR, OLIVE, 4 SIZES, ZINC LID, COMMON.
ATLAS MASON	-ATLAS- MASON'S PATENT	ATLAS MASON
20.00-30.00	OLIVE 12.00-15.00 BLUE 12.00-15.00	OLIVE 10.00-12.00 OTHER 1.00- 2.00

ATLAS	ATLAS	ATLAS
MACHINE MADE, CLEAR, 4 SIZES, ZINC LID. COMMON.	MACHINE MADE, CLEAR, OLIVE, 3 SIZES, ZINC LID.	MACHINE MADE, CLEAR, AQUA, 3 SIZES, GLASS LID, ZINC BAND.
ATLAS (A logo)	ATLAS (A logo) MASON	ATLAS MASON IMPROVED PAT'D
1.00-2.00	OLIVE 18.00-20.00 OTHER 2.00-4.00	6.00-8.00

ATLAS	ATLAS	ATLAS
MACHINE MADE, AQUA, 3 SIZES, ZINC LID.	MACHINE MADE, CLEAR, AQUA, 3 SIZES, ZINC LID.	MACHINE MADE, AQUA, 3 SIZES, METAL LID.
-ATLAS- MASON'S PATENT NOV 30TH 1858	ATLAS SPECIAL	ATLAS SPECIAL MASON
3.00-5.00	AQUA 3.00-5.00 GREEN 12.00-15.00 BLUE 15.00-18.00	3.00-5.00

ATLAS	ATLAS	ATLAS
MACHINE MADE, AQUA, CLEAR 4 SIZES, ZINC LID.	MACHINE MADE, CLEAR, AQUA, OLIVE, QUART, ZINC LID.	MACHINE MADE, CLEAR, 3 SIZES, ZINC LID, WIRE BAIL.
ATLAS STRONG SHOULDER MASON	• ATLAS • STRONG SHOULDER MASON	ATLAS WHOLE FRUIT JAR
OLIVE 20.00-25.00 BLUE 18.00-20.00	OLIVE 12.00-15.00 OTHER 1.00-2.00	1.00-2.00
ATTERBURY	AUTOMATIC SEALER	B & B
HANDMADE, AQUA, QUART, TAPERED STOPPER.	HANDMADE, AQUA, 3 SIZES, GLASS LID, SPRING CLIP.	MACHINE MADE, AMBER, QUART, PINT, GLASS LID, METAL BAND.
ATTERBURY	THE AUTOMATIC SEALER	B&B
325.00-350.00	90.00-100.00	2.00-3.00
J. C. BAKER'S	BAKER BROS.	BALL
HANDMADE, AQUA, QUART, GLASS LID, IRON YOKE.	HANDMADE, AQUA, QUART, WAX SEALER, CRUDE.	HANDMADE, GREEN, 3 SIZES, ZINC LID.
J.C. BAKER'S PATENT AUG 14 1860	NO SIDE DESIGN BOTTOM READS: "BAKER BROS. BALTO. MD."	Ball
125.00-150.00	30.00-35.00	1.00-2.00
BALL	BALL	BALL
MACHINE MADE, CLEAR, QUART	HANDMADE, AQUA, 3 SIZES, ZINC LID.	MACHINE MADE, CLEAR, 3 SIZES, GLASS LID, WIRE BAIL.
Ball	Ball	BALL DELUXE JAR
1.00-2.00	3.00-5.00	2.00-4.00

BALL HANDMADE, AQUA, 3 SIZES, GLASS LID, GROUND TOP. *The Ball* PAT APL'D FOR 45.00-50.00	**BALL** HANDMADE, CLEAR, QUART GLASS LID, WIRE BAIL, SQUARE *Ball* ECLIPSE 1.00-2.00	**BALL** MACHINE MADE, CLEAR, 4 SIZES, ROUNDED SQUARE, GLASS LID, WIRE BAIL. *Ball* ECLIPSE 1.00-2.00
BALL MACHINE MADE, CLEAR, 3 SIZES, ROUNDED SQUARE, GLASS LID, WIRE BAIL. *Ball* ECLIPSE 1.00-2.00	**BALL** MACHINE MADE, CLEAR, 3 SIZES, ROUNDED SQUARE, GLASS LID, WIRE BAIL. *Ball* ECLIPSE WIDE MOUTH 1.00-2.00	**BALL** MACHINE MADE, CLEAR, AQUA, 3 SIZES, GLASS LID, WIRE BAIL. *Ball* IDEAL 1.00-2.00
BALL MACHINE MADE, CLEAR, AQUA, 3 SIZES, GLASS LID, WIRE BAIL. *Ball* IDEAL 1.00-2.00	**BALL** MACHINE MADE, CLEAR, 3 SIZES, GLASS LID, WIRE BAIL. *Ball* IDEAL MADE IN U.S.A. 1.00-2.00	**BALL (DATE ERROR)** MACHINE MADE, AQUA, QUART, GLASS LID, WIRE BAIL. *Ball* IDEAL PAT D JULY 14 1988 2.00-3.00
BALL MACHINE MADE, CLEAR, AQUA, 3 SIZES, GLASS LID, WIRE BAIL. *Ball* IDEAL 1.00-2.00	**BALL** MACHINE MADE, CLEAR, BLUE, 3 SIZES, GLASS LID, (DATE ON BACK) PAT'D JULY 14, 1908 *Ball* IDEAL 3.00-5.00	**BALL** MACHINE MADE, CLEAR, BLUE, 4 SIZES, GLASS LID. *Ball* IDEAL PAT D JULY 14 1908 2.00-4.00

BALL MACHINE MADE, CLEAR, HALF GALLON. PROPERTY OF SOUTHERN METHODIST ORPHANS HOME WACO, TEXAS 20.00-25.00	**BALL** MACHINE MADE, AQUA, 3 SIZES, GLASS LID, METAL BAND. *Ball* IMPROVED 1.00-3.00	**BALL** MACHINE MADE, AQUA, 3 SIZES, GLASS LID, METAL BAND. *Ball* IMPROVED MASON PATENT 2.00-4.00
BALL MACHINE MADE, AQUA, 3 SIZES, METAL BAND. *Ball* IMPROVED MASON PATENT 1858 2.00-4.00	**BALL** MACHINE MADE, AQUA, 2 SIZES, ZINC LID. THE BALL JAR MASON'S PATENT NOV 30TH 1858 4.00-6.00	**BALL** HANDMADE, AQUA, OLIVE, 3 SIZES, ZINC LID, GROUND LIP. *Ball* MASON OLIVE 15.00-18.00 OTHER 1.00-2.00
BALL (OTHER VARIATIONS) *Ball* MASON *Ball* MASON 1.00-3.00	**BALL (ERROR)** HANDMADE, AQUA, QUART, ZINC LID. *Ball* MAZON 2.00-3.00	**BALL** MACHINE MADE, CLEAR, AQUA, GLASS LID, ZINC BAND. *Ball* MASON IMPROVED 1.00-2.00
BALL MACHINE MADE, AQUA, 3 SIZES, ZINC LID. THE *Ball Mason* 3.00-5.00	**BALL** MACHINE MADE, CLEAR, AQUA, 3 SIZES, ZINC LID. *Ball* MASON'S PATENT 3.00-5.00	**BALL** HANDMADE, GREEN, 3 SIZES, ZINC LID, GROUND LIP. *Ball* MASON'S PATENT 1858 2.00-4.00

BALL HANDMADE, GREEN, 3 SIZES, ZINC LID, GROUND LIP. *Ball* MASON'S PATENT 1858 2.00-4.00	**BALL** HANDMADE, GREEN, QUART, ZINC LID, GROUND LIP. *The Ball* MASON'S PATENT 1858 3.00-5.00	**BALL** HANDMADE, AQUA, QUART, ZINC LID, GROUND LIP. *Ball* MASON'S PATENT NOV 30TH 1858 3.00-5.00
BALL HANDMADE, GREEN, BLUE, QUART, ZINC LID, GROUND LIP. THE BALL MASON'S PATENT 1858 3.00-5.00	**BALL** HANDMADE, GREEN, QUART, ZINC LID, GROUND LIP. *Ball* MASON'S PATENT 1858 4.00-6.00	**BALL** HANDMADE, AQUA, QUART, GROUND LIP, ZINC LID. BALL MASON'S PATENT NOV 30TH 1858 3.00-5.00
BALL (ERROR) HANDMADE, AQUA, QUART, ZINC LID. *Ball* MASON'S PATENT NOV. 80TH 1858 6.00-8.00	**BALL** MACHINE MADE, CLEAR, AQUA, 4 SIZES, ZINC LID. *Ball* PERFECT MASON 1.00-2.00	**BALL** HANDMADE, AQUA, CLEAR, 1 PT. 1 QT. ZINC LID. *Ball* PERFECT MASON 1.00-2.00
BALL MACHINE MADE, GREEN 7 INCHES TALL, SCREW TOP. *BALL* PERFECT MASON 2.00-4.00	**BALL** MACHINE MADE, CLEAR, AQUA, 4 SIZES, ZINC LID. *Ball* PERFECT MASON 1.00-2.00	**BALL** HANDMADE, AQUA, QUART, GLASS LID, ZINC BAND. *Ball* PERFECTION 12.00-15.00

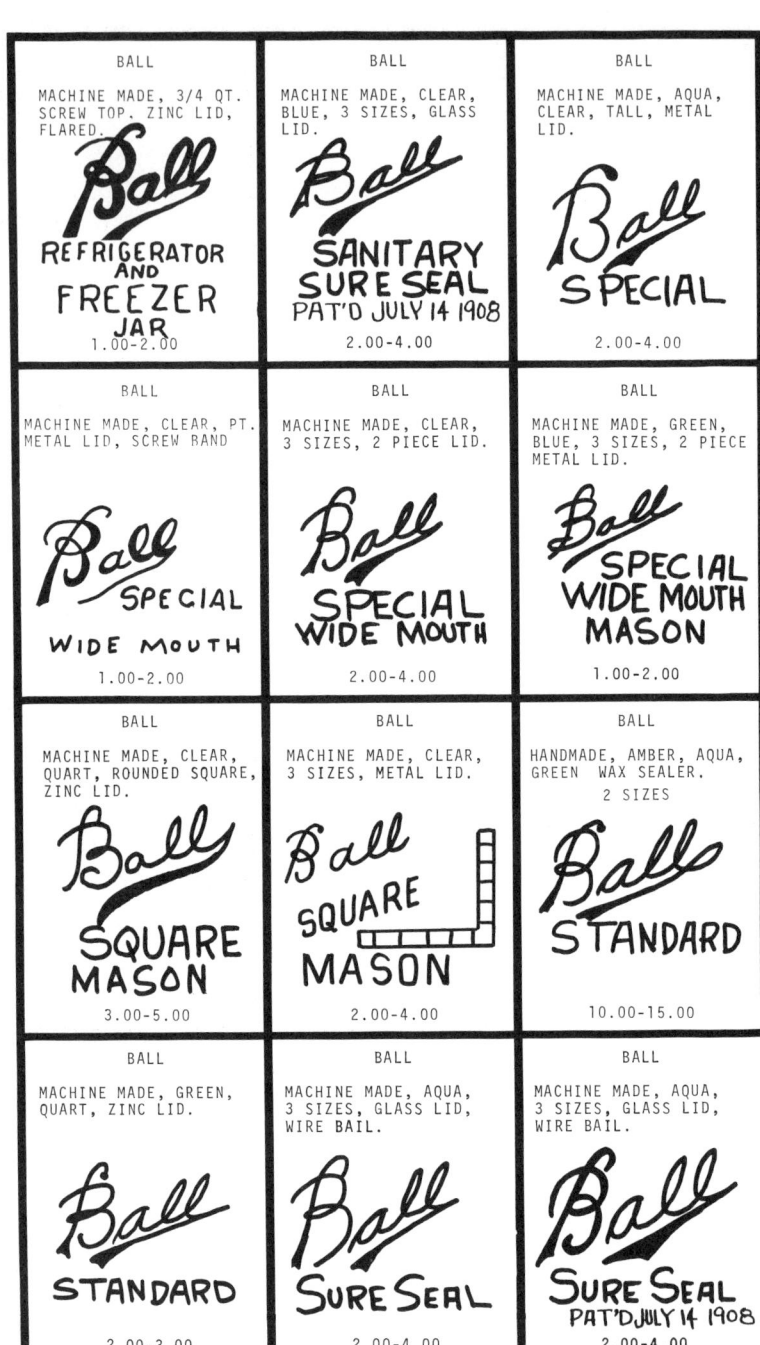

BALL MACHINE MADE, AQUA, 3 SIZES, GLASS LID, WIRE BAIL.  2.00-4.00	**BBGM CO.** HANDMADE, BLUE, GREEN, GLASS LID, METAL SCREW BAND.  25.00-30.00	**BBGM CO.** HANDMADE, BLUE, GREEN, QUART, GLASS LID, METAL SCREW BAND.  25.00-30.00
BBGM CO. HANDMADE, BLUE, GREEN, QUART, GLASS LID, WIRE BAIL.  25.00-30.00	**BBGM CO.** HANDMADE, GREEN, 3 SIZES, GROUND LIP, ZINC LID.  35.00-40.00	**BALTIMORE GLASS WORKS** HANDMADE, AQUA, QUART, APPLIED LID. BALTIMORE GLASS WORKS 175.00-200.00
BANNER MACHINE MADE, CLEAR, 3 SIZES, GLASS LID, WIRE BAIL.  8.00-10.00	**BANNER** MACHINE MADE, CLEAR, 3 SIZES, GLASS LID, WIRE BAIL.  8.00-10.00	**BANNER** MACHINE MADE, CLEAR, 3 SIZES, GLASS LID, WIRE BAIL.  10.00-12.00
BANNER MACHINE MADE, AQUA, 3 SIZES, GLASS LID, WIRE BAIL.  8.00-10.00	**BAMBERGER'S MASON JAR** MACHINE MADE, BALL BLUE 3 SIZES, GLASS LID, WIRE BAIL.  8.00-10.00	**BENTON MYERS** MACHINE MADE, CLEAR, 3 SIZES, TOP UNKNOWN. BASE READS: "BENTON MEYERS & CO. CLEVELAND OHIO." 6.00-8.00

BEAVER HANDMADE, CLEAR, AQUA, GLASS LID, WIRE BAIL.  18.00-20.00	BEAVER HANDMADE, CLEAR, AMBER, GREEN, GLASS LID, METAL BAND.  MIDGET 50.00-75.00 AMBER 350.00-400.00 OTHER 25.00-30.00	BEAVER MACHINE MADE, CLEAR, AQUA, 3 SIZES, GLASS LID, METAL BAND. BEAVER 50.00-60.00
BEE HIVE MACHINE MADE, CLEAR 3 SIZES, GLASS LID, METAL BAND.  85.00-100.00	BENNETT'S NO. 1 MACHINE MADE, CLEAR, AQUA, QUART, ZINC LID BENNETT'S NO.1 150.00-200.00	BENNETT'S NO. 2 HANDMADE, GREEN, QUART CLOSURE UNKNOWN. BENNETT'S NO2 225.00-250.00
BENNETT'S NO.2 (ERROR) HANDMADE, AQUA, QUART, CLOSURE UNKNOWN. BENNETT'S No S 375.00-400.00	BERNARDIN MASON MACHINE MADE, CLEAR, 3 SIZES, METAL LID. Bernardin MASON 1.00-3.00	BEST MACHINE MADE, AQUA, QUART, GLASS LID, METAL BAND. BEST 20.00-25.00
THE BEST HANDMADE, LIGHT GREEN, QUART, GLASS STOPPER. LID: AUG. 18TH. 1868 THE BEST 250.00-300.00	THE BEST FRUIT KEEPER HANDMADE, AQUA, QUART, GLASS LID, METAL CLIP. "The Best" FRUITKEEPER 30.00-40.00	BEST WIDE MOUTH MACHINE MADE, AQUA, CLEAR, 4 SIZES, ZINC LID. Best WIDE MOUTH 1.00-2.00

BEST WIDE MOUTH MACHINE MADE, CLEAR, AQUA, 3 SIZES, ZINC LID, *Best* WIDE MOUTH MADE IN CANADA 1.00-2.00	**BLUE RIBBON** CLEAR W/BUBBLES, QUART GLASS LID, WIRE CLIP. *BLUE RIBBON* 6.00-8.00	**BGCO** HANDMADE, AMBER, QUART, WAX SEAL. BGCo (ON BOTTOM) AQUA 10.00-12.00 AMBER 85.00-100.00
F & J BODINE HANDMADE, AQUA, PINT, QUART, GLASS LID, CLAMP F&J BODINE PHILADA 75.00-100.00	**BOLDT MASON** MACHINE MADE, AQUA, BLUE, 3 SIZES, ZINC LID. BOLDT MASON 18.00-20.00	**BOLDT MASON JAR** MACHINE MADE, AQUA, BLUE, 3 SIZES, ZINC LID. BOLDT MASON JAR 18.00-20.00
BOSCO DOUBLE SEAL MACHINE MADE, CLEAR, QUART, GLASS LID, WIRE BAIL. Bosco Double Seal 4.00-6.00	**BOSTWICK** CLEAR, 1 PT. GLASS LID, METAL CLAMP. The Bostwick Perfect Sealer 35.00-40.00	**BOYD MASON** MACHINE MADE, CLEAR, AQUA, OLIVE, 3 SIZES, ZINC LID. Boyds MASON OLIVE 15.00-18.00 OTHER 4.00-6.00
GENUINE BOYDS MASON HANDMADE, GREEN, QUART, ZINC LID. GENUINE Boyds MASON 4.00-6.00	**GENUINE BOYDS MASON** MACHINE MADE, CLEAR, 3 SIZES, ZINC LID. GENUINE Boyds MASON 4.00-6.00	**BOYDS MASON** HANDMADE, GREEN, QUART, ZINC LID, GROUND LIP. Boyds MASON 4.00-6.00

BOYD PERFECT MASON	BOYD PERFECT MASON	BOYD'S PERFECT MASON
MACHINE MADE, CLEAR, 3 SIZES, ZINC LID.	MACHINE MADE, CLEAR, AQUA 3 SIZES, ZINC LID.	MACHINE MADE, CLEAR, 3 SIZES, ZINC LID.
BOYDS PERFECT MASON	BOYD PERFECT MASON	Boyds PERFECT MASON
2.00-4.00	2.00-4.00	4.00-6.00
BRAUN SAFETEE MASON	THE BRELLE JAR	BRIGHTON
MACHINE MADE, CLEAR, 3 SIZES, ZINC LID.	MACHINE MADE, CLEAR, 3 SIZES, GLASS LID, CLIP.	HANDMADE, CLEAR, QUART, GLASS LID, TOGGLE.
BRAUN Safetee MASON	The Brelle JAR	BRIGHTON
2.00-4.00	15.00-20.00	50.00-60.00
BROCKWAY CLEAR-VU MASON	BROCKWAY SUR-GRIP MASON	BUCKEYE
MACHINE MADE, CLEAR, 4 SIZES, METAL LID.	MACHINE MADE, CLEAR, 3 SIZES, METAL LID.	HANDMADE, AQUA, QUART, GLASS LID, IRON YOKE.
Brockway CLEAR-VU MASON	Brockway SUR-GRIP MASON	BUCKEYE
1.00-3.00	1.00-2.00	150.00-160.00
BULACH	BULACH	THE BURLINGTON
HANDMADE, OLIVE, QUART, GLASS LID, METAL CLAMP.	MACHINE MADE, GREEN, QUART, GLASS LID, WIRE CLIP.	HANDMADE, CLEAR, AQUA, 3 SIZES, GLASS LID, METAL BAND.
BULACH	BULACH	THE BURLINGTON B.G. CO R'D 1876
10.00-12.00	1.00-2.00	40.00-50.00

C.C. CO. CLEAR, 2 QUART, 10 1/2" TALL, GLASS TOP, WIRE CLAMP, 5" SQUARE INDENTATION ON BACK. C.C.CO 4.00-6.00	**CHATTANOOGA MASON** MACHINE MADE, CLEAR, 3 SIZES, ZINC LID. Ⓒ 4.00-6.00	**CADIZ JAR** HANDMADE, AQUA, QUART, GLASS THREADED LID. CADIZ JAR 125.00-150.00
CALCUTT'S HANDMADE, CLEAR, AQUA, QUART, GLASS SCREW LID, GROUND LIP. LID READS: "CALCUTT'S PAT APRIL 11 & NOV 7, 1893" 35.00-40.00	**CANADA** MACHINE MADE, GREEN, 3 SIZES, GLASS LID, ZINC BAND. CANADA (compass N/W/E/S) TRADE MARK 300.00 +	**CANADIAN JEWEL** MACHINE MADE, CLEAR, 4 SIZES, GLASS LID, METAL BAND. Canadian JEWEL MADE IN CANADA 1.00-2.00
CANADIAN KING MACHINE MADE, CLEAR, 3 SIZES, GLASS LID. MADE IN CANADA Canadian King WIDE MOUTH 20.00-25.00	**CANADIAN MASON JAR** MACHINE MADE, CLEAR, 3 SIZES, METAL LID. CANADIAN MASON JAR MADE IN CANADA 1.00-2.00	**CANADIAN SURE SEAL** MACHINE MADE, CLEAR, 3 SIZES, METAL LID. CANADIAN SURE SEAL MADE IN CANADA 2.00-3.00
THE CANTON DOMESTIC HANDMADE, CLEAR, QUART, GLASS LID, WIRE BAIL. THE CANTON DOMESTIC FRUIT JAR 50.00-75.00	**CARROLLS** MACHINE MADE, CLEAR, 3 SIZES, GLASS LID, WIRE BAIL. CARROLLS TRUE SEAL 8.00-10.00	**CASSIDY** HANDMADE, AQUA, QUART, GLASS LID, UNIQUE WIRE BAIL. CASSIDY 150.00-175.00

C F J CO. HANDMADE, GREEN, QUART, GLASS LID, METAL BAND.  12.00-15.00	**C G CO** HANDMADE, AQUA, QUART, ZINC LID, GROUND LIP.  12.00-15.00	**A & D H CHAMBERS** HANDMADE, AQUA, QUART, WAX SEAL, RARE.  50.00-60.00
THE CHAMPION HANDMADE, AQUA, QUART, GLASS LID, IRON SCREW YOKE.  THE CHAMPION PAT AUG 31, 1869 100.00-125.00	**CHAMPION SYRUP** HANDMADE, AQUA, QUART, ZINC LID. CHAMPION SYRUP REFINING CO. INDIANAPOLIS 20.00-25.00	**CHEF** MACHINE MADE, CLEAR, 4 SIZES, GLASS LID, WIRE BAIL. CHEF 4.00-6.00
CHEF MACHINE MADE, CLEAR, 4 SIZES, GLASS LID, WIRE BAIL.  4.00-6.00	**THE CHIEF** HANDMADE, AQUA, QUART, GLASS LID, UNIQUE LOCKING BAR. THE CHIEF 175.00-200.00	**CLARK FRUIT JAR CO.** HANDMADE, BLUE, GREEN, 3 SIZES, GLASS LID, UNIQUE CAM LEVER. CLARKE FRUIT JAR CLEVELAND, O. 45.00-55.00
CLARK'S PEERLESS HANDMADE, AQUA, CLEAR, 2 SIZES, GLASS LID, WIRE BAIL. CLARK'S PEERLESS 10.00-12.00	**CLARKS PEERLESS** MACHINE MADE, AQUA, 3 SIZES, GLASS LID.  8.00-10.00	**CLEVELAND FRUIT JUICE CO.** MACHINE MADE, CLEAR, QUART, GLASS LID, WIRE BAIL. BOTTOM: "CLEVELAND FRUIT JUICE CO." 6.00-8.00

CLIMAX MACHINE MADE, CLEAR, 3 SIZES, GREEN, GLASS LID. *TRADE MARK* **CLIMAX** *REGISTERED* 3.00-5.00	**CLYDE GLASS WORKS** HANDMADE, CLEAR, GREEN, QUART, GLASS LID, WIRE BAIL. ON LID: "CLYDE GLASS WORKS. CLYDE, N.Y." 12.00-15.00	**CLYDE MASON** HANDMADE, GREEN, QUART, ZINC LID, GROUND LIP. **CLYDE MASON** 15.00-20.00
THE CLYDE HANDMADE, CLEAR, GREEN, QUART, GLASS LID. PINT WIRE BAIL *The Clyde* 8.00-10.00	**CLYDE IMPROVED MASON** HANDMADE, GREEN, QUART, GLASS LID, METAL BAND. **CLYDE IMPROVED MASON** 10.00-12.00	**COHANSEY** HANDMADE, BLUE, QUART, BARREL DESIGN, CORK TOP GLASS MF'G CO. **COHANSEY** 90.00-100.00
COHANSEY HANDMADE, AQUA, QUART, GLASS LID, WIRE RING, BARREL DESIGN **COHANSEY** 15.00-20.00	**COHANSEY** HANDMADE, BARREL DESIGN AQUA, QUART, WAX SEAL GLASS MFG Co **COHANSEY** PAT MAR 20, 77 100.00-125.00	**COLLINS & CHAPMAN** AQUA, QUART, BAND AROUND THE MOUTH. COLLINS & CHAPMAN WHEELING, W.V. 500.00-600.00
COLUMBIA MACHINE MADE, AMETHYST, QUART, GLASS LID, METAL CLAMP *Columbia* MADE IN CANADA 20.00-25.00	**COLUMBIA** HANDMADE, AQUA, CLEAR, 3 SIZES, GLASS LID, WIRE CLIP. **COLUMBIA** 20.00-25.00	**CONSERVE** HANDMADE, CLEAR, QUART, GLASS LID, WIRE BAIL. **CONSERVE JAR** 6.00-8.00

CORONA MACHINE MADE, CLEAR, 3 SIZES, GLASS LID, ZINC BAND. IMPROVED CORONA MADE IN CANADA 1.00-2.00	CORONA MACHINE MADE, CLEAR, 4 SIZES, GLASS LID, ZINC BAND. CORONA JAR MADE IN CANADA 2.00-3.00	CORONA MACHINE MADE, CLEAR, 4 SIZES, GLASS LID, ZINC BAND. IMPROVED CORONA JAR MADE IN CANADA 1.00-2.00
CORONET HANDMADE, CLEAR, 3 SIZES, GLASS LID, ZINC BAND.  50.00-75.00	CROWN (MADE IN CANADA) WE HAVE MORE THAN 50 DIFFERENT CROWN JARS. SINCE THESE ARE SUCH NICE JARS, A COLLECTION MADE UP OF THE DIFFERENT SIZES & TYPES IS QUITE REWARDING. MOST OF THE CROWNS HAVE GLASS LIDS. A FEW ARE SHOWN AT THE RIGHT. THEY RANGE IN PRICE FROM $2.00-20.00	CROWN  
CROWN 	CROWN CORDIAL & EXTRACT HANDMADE, CLEAR, GREEN, 3 SIZES, GLASS LID, WIRE BAIL.  NEW YORK 10.00-12.00	CROWN MASON MACHINE MADE, CLEAR, 4 SIZES, ZINC LID. CROWN MASON 1.00-2.00
CROWN MASON MACHINE MADE, CLEAR, 3 SIZES, ZINC LID. CROWN MASON 1.00-2.00	CRYSTAL HANDMADE, AQUA, QUART, GLASS THREADED CAP. CRYSTAL 50.00-55.00	CRYSTAL JAR HANDMADE, CLEAR, AMETHYST, QUART, GLASS LID. CRYSTAL JAR 25.00-30.00

CRYSTAL JAR C G HANDMADE, CLEAR, QUART, GLASS SCREW LID. **CRYSTAL JAR CG** 25.00-50.00	**CRYSTAL** HANDMADE, CLEAR, PINT, QUART, ZINC LID. *Crystal* MASON 6.00-8.00	**CUNNINGHAM & IHMSEN** HANDMADE, AQUA, QUART, WAX SEAL. CUNNINGHAM & IHMSEN 20.00-25.00
CUNNINGHAM & SON HANDMADE, AQUA, QUART, WAX SEAL. ON BOTTOM: "CUNNINGHAM & SON" 20.00-25.00	**CUNNINGHAM'S & CO.** HANDMADE, AQUA, QUART, WAX SEAL. ON BOTTOM: "CUNNINGHAM'S & CO." 20.00-25.00	**CURTIS & MOORE** HANDMADE, CLEAR, QUART, GLASS LID, WIRE BAIL. CURTIS & MOORE TRADE MARK BOSTON, MASS. 20.00-25.00
THE DAISY HANDMADE, CLEAR, QUART, GLASS LID, WIRE BAIL. THE DAISY F.E. WARD & CO 10.00-12.00	**THE DAISY JAR** HANDMADE, CLEAR, QUART, GLASS LID, METAL CLIP. THE DAISY JAR 125.00-150.00	**R. M. DALBEY'S** HANDMADE, AQUA, 2 SIZES, METAL LID, THUMBSCREWS. R.M. DALBEY'S FRUIT JAR PAT. NOV 16 1858 500.00 +
DALBEY'S FRUIT JAR HANDMADE, GREEN, QUART, METAL LID, THUMBSCREWS. DALBEY'S FRUIT JAR PAT NOV 16 1858 500.00 +	**DALBEYS FRUIT JAR** HANDMADE, GREEN, QUART, GLASS LID WITH YOKE. PATENTED BY RM DALBEY JUNE 6TH 1866 200.00-275.00	**THE DANDY** HANDMADE, CLEAR, AQUA, AMBER, 3 SIZES, GLASS LID, WIRE BAIL. TRADE MARK THE DANDY AMBER 75.00-90.00 OTHER 30.00-35.00

THE DARLING HANDMADE, AQUA, 2 SIZES, GLASS LID, METAL BAND.  25.00-30.00	**THE DARLING IMPERIAL** HANDMADE, AQUA, 2 SIZES, GLASS LID, METAL BAND.  30.00-35.00	**DECKER DEPENDABLE** MACHINE MADE, CLEAR, 2 SIZES, METAL LID.  1.00-3.00
DECKER'S IOWANA MACHINE MADE, CLEAR, 3 SIZES, GLASS LID, WIRE BAIL. 3.00-5.00	**DECKERS IOWANA** MACHINE MADE, CLEAR, PINT, QUART, GLASS LID 2.00-3.00	**DECKER'S VICTOR** MACHINE MADE, CLEAR, 3 SIZES, GLASS LID, WIRE BAIL.  3.00-5.00
DEXTER HANDMADE, AQUA, QUART, GLASS LID, WIRE BAIL. 55.00-60.00	**DEXTER** HANDMADE, AQUA, QUART, GLASS LID, SCREW BAND. 25.00-30.00	**D G CO** HANDMADE, CLEAR, PINT, GLASS LID, SCREW BAND.  35.00-40.00
DIAMOND FRUIT JAR MACHINE MADE, CLEAR, 3 SIZES, GLASS LID, SCREW BAND. 3.00-5.00	**IMPROVED DIAMOND JAR** MACHINE MADE, CLEAR, 3 SIZES, GLASS LID, WIRE BAIL. 3.00-5.00	**THE DICTATOR** HANDMADE, AQUA, QUART, WAX SEAL. 70.00-75.00

DICTATOR D HANDMADE, AQUA, QUART, METAL LID, CLIP. *DICTATOR* *D* BACK READS: "D. I. HOLCOMB-DEC. 14th. 1869" 75.00-100.00	**DILLON** HANDMADE, AQUA, QUART, WAX SEAL. BOTTOM READS: "DILLON & CO. FAIRMOUNT, IND." 10.00-12.00	**D O C** HANDMADE, AQUA, QUART, WAX SEAL. *DOC* 12.00-15.00
DODGE-SWEENEY & CO. HANDMADE, AQUA, CLEAR, 2 SIZES, GLASS LID, METAL BAND. *DODGE-SWEENEY CO* *CALIFORNIA* *BUTTER* 40.00-45.00	**DOMINION** HANDMADE, CLEAR, 3 SIZES, GLASS LID, METAL BAND. *DOMINION* 75.00-100.00	**DOMINION MASON** MACHINE MADE, CLEAR, 3 SIZES, ZINC LID. *Dominion* *MASON* 1.00-3.00
DOMINION MASON MACHINE MADE, CLEAR, 3 SIZES, GLASS LID, WIRE BAIL. *Dominion* *MASON* *MADE IN CANADA* 1.00-2.00	**DOMINION SPECIAL** MACHINE MADE, CLEAR, 3 SIZES, METAL LID. *Dominion* *Wide Mouth* *SPECIAL* 1.00-2.00	**DOMINION WIDE MOUTH SPECIAL** MACHINE MADE, CLEAR, 3 SIZES, METAL LID. *Dominion* *Wide Mouth* *SPECIAL* *MADE IN CANADA* 1.00-2.00
DOOLITTLE HANDMADE, AQUA, QUART, GLASS LID, UNIQUE METAL HOOK. *DOOLITTLE* 30.00-35.00	**DOOLITTLE** HANDMADE, AQUA, QUART, GLASS LID, UNIQUE METAL HOOKS. *DOOLITTLE* *THE* *SELF SEALER* 50.00-75.00	**DOUBLE SAFETY** MACHINE MADE, CLEAR, 4 SIZES, GLASS LID, WIRE BAIL. *Double* *Safety* 3.00-5.00

DOUBLE SEAL MACHINE MADE, CLEAR, 3 SIZES, GLASS LID, WIRE BAIL *Double Seal* 3.00-5.00	**DREY EVER SEAL** MACHINE MADE, CLEAR, 4 SIZES, GLASS LID, WIRE BAIL. *Drey EVER SEAL* 1.00-2.00	**DREY IMPROVED EVER SEAL** MACHINE MADE, CLEAR, 4 SIZES, GLASS LID, WIRE BAIL. *Drey* Pat'd 1920 IMPROVED EVER SEAL 2.00-3.00
DREY IMPROVED EVER SEAL MACHINE MADE, CLEAR, 4 SIZES, GLASS LID, WIRE BAIL. *Drey* IMPROVED EVER SEAL 1.00-2.00	**DREY MASON** MACHINE MADE, CLEAR, 3 SIZES, GREEN, ZINC LID. *Drey* MASON 1.00-2.00	**DREY PERFECT MASON** MACHINE MADE, CLEAR, AQUA, AMBER, 4 SIZES, ZINC LID. *Drey* PERFECT MASON AMBER 18.00-20.00 OTHER 1.00-2.00
DREY PERFECT MASON MACHINE MADE, CLEAR, 3 SIZES, ZINC LID. *Drey* PERFECT MASON 1.00-2.00	**DREY SQUARE MASON** MACHINE MADE, CLEAR, 3 SIZES, ZINC LID. *Drey* SQUARE MASON 2.00-3.00	**DUNKLEY** MACHINE MADE, CLEAR, QUART, HINGED GLASS LID. DUNKLEY PAT? SEPT 20, 98 KALAMAZOO 4.00-6.00
DUNKLEY MACHINE MADE, CLEAR, QUART, HINGED GLASS LID. DUNKLEY PAT? SEPT 20, 98 APR. 30, 01 4.00-6.00	**DUR FOR (FRENCH)** MACHINE MADE, DARK GREEN, QUART, GLASS LID, HINGED. DUR FOR 1.00-2.00	**DURHAM** MACHINE MADE, GREEN, 3 SIZES, GLASS LID, WIRE BAIL. DURHAM 12.00-15.00

DYSON'S MACHINE MADE, CLEAR, QUART, GLASS LID, WIRE BAIL. DYSON'S ✠ PURE FOOD PRODUCTS 15.00-18.00	**EAGLE** HANDMADE, GREEN, QUART, WAX SEAL. EAGLE 70.00-75.00	**EAGLE** HANDMADE, AQUA, QUART, GLASS LID, IRON YOKE. PAT DEC. 28TH 1858 EAGLE REISE JUNE 16TH 1868 85.00-95.00
EASY HANDMADE, CLEAR, QUART GLASS LID, WIRE CLAMP. EASY CO TRADE MARK VACUUM JAR 20.00-25.00	**THE ECLIPSE** HANDMADE, LIGHT GREEN, 2 SIZES, WAX SEAL. THE ECLIPSE 85.00-95.00	**THE ECLIPSE** HANDMADE, AQUA, QUART, WAX SEAL. THE ECLIPSE WAX SEALER 75.00-85.00
ECLIPSE JAR HANDMADE, LIGHT GREEN, QUART, THREADED GLASS LID. ECLIPSE JAR 150.00-175.00	**ECONOMY** HANDMADE, AQUA, QUART, WAX SEAL. ECONOMY SEALER PAT.º SEPT 13TH 1858 20.00-25.00	**ECONOMY** HANDMADE, AQUA, QUART, GLASS DOMED LID, WIRE BAIL. ECONOMY SEALER PATº SEPT 15TH 1885 85.00-100.00
ECONOMY MACHINE MADE, CLEAR, 3 SIZES, METAL LID, SPRING CLIP. Economy TRADE MARK 2.00-4.00	**ECONOMY** MACHINE MADE, CLEAR, 3 SIZES, METAL LID, SPRING CLIP. Economy TRADE MARK 2.00-4.00	**ECONOMY** AMBER, PINT, METAL LID, SPRING CLIP. Economy 3.00-5.00

ECONOMY AMETHYST, METAL LID, SPRING CLIP. *Economy* **TRADE MARK** 3.00-5.00	**E G CO** HANDMADE, AMBER, AQUA, QUART, ZINC LID. E.G. Cº (ON BASE) AMBER 40.00-50.00 AQUA 18.00-22.00	**ELECTRIC** HANDMADE, AQUA, QUART, GLASS LID, WIRE BAIL. TRADE MARK **ELECTRIC** 10.00-12.00
ELECTRIC MACHINE MADE, AQUA, 3 SIZES, GLASS LID, WIRE BAIL. *Electric* **TRADE MARK** 8.00-10.00	**ELECTRIC FRUIT JAR** HANDMADE, AQUA, QUART, GLASS LID, UNIQUE CLAMP. ELECTRIC FRUIT JAR (globe logo) 60.00-70.00	**N W ELECTROGLAS** MACHINE MADE, CLEAR, 3 SIZES, ZINC LID. **NW ELECTROGLAS** 2.00-4.00
EMPIRE HANDMADE, AQUA, BLUE, QUART, STOPPER NECK. **EMPIRE** 200.00-250.00	**EMPIRE** MACHINE MADE, CLEAR, 4 SIZES, GLASS LID, WIRE BAIL. (cross with EMPIRE) 8.00-10.00	**THE EMPIRE** HANDMADE, AQUA, QUART, GLASS LID, CAM LEVER. **THE EMPIRE** 60.00-70.00
EMPRESS HANDMADE, AQUA, QUART, GLASS LID, ZINC BAND. **EMPRESS** 100.00-150.00	**ERIE** HANDMADE, CLEAR, 2 SIZES, GLASS LID, ZINC BAND. ERIE (E in hexagon) FRUIT JAR 100.00-125.00	**ERIE** HANDMADE, CLEAR, QUART, GLASS LID, METAL BAND. BASE READS: "ERIE" 12.00-15.00

ERIE LIGHTING MACHINE MADE, CLEAR, 3 SIZES, GLASS LID, WIRE BAIL. *ERIE LIGHTNING* 20.00-25.00	**EUREKA** HANDMADE, CLEAR, AQUA, QUART, TAPERED LID, RARE. *EUREKA PATᵈ DEC 27ᵀᴴ 1864* 75.00-100.00	**EUREKA** MACHINE MADE, CLEAR, 2 SIZES, GLASS LID, SPRING STRAP. *Eureka* 12.00-15.00
EVERLASTING JAR MACHINE MADE, CLEAR, GREEN, 3 SIZES, GLASS LID, TOGGLES. *Everlasting JAR* 15.00-20.00	**IMPROVED JAR EVERLASTING** MACHINE MADE, CLEAR, 3 SIZES, GLASS LID, TOGGLES. *IMPROVED Everlasting JAR* 12.00-15.00	**IMPROVED JAR EVERLASTING** MACHINE MADE, CLEAR, PINT, QUART, GLASS LID, TOGGLES. *IMPROVED EVERLASTING JAR* 15.00-20.00
EXCELSIOR HANDMADE, AQUA, QUART, GLASS LID, SCREW BAND. EXCELSIOR 90.00-100.00	**EXCELSIOR IMPROVED** HANDMADE, AQUA, QUART, GLASS LID, SCREW BAND. EXCELSIOR IMPROVED 40.00-50.00	**EXWACO** HANDMADE, MILK GLASS, LIGHT GREEN, PINT, GLASS LID, ZINC BAND. EX WACO 10.00-12.00
F A & CO HANDMADE, AQUA, QUART, PONTILED BASE, RARE. BASE READS: "F A & CO." 125.00-150.00	**F & S** MACHINE MADE, AQUA, GLASS LID, WIRE BAIL *F&S* 8.00-10.00	**FB CO.** HANDMADE, AQUA, QUART, WAX SEAL, CRUDE. BASE READS: "FB CO." 10.00-12.00

F C G CO. HANDMADE, AMBER, AQUA, QUART, WAX SEAL. BOTTOM READS: "F C G CO." AMBER 85.00-100.00 AQUA 15.00-18.00	**FAHNSTOCK ALBREE & CO.** HANDMADE, GREEN, QUART, STOPPER TOP. BASE READS: "FAHNSTOCK ALBREE & CO" 70.00-80.00	**FAHNSTOCK FORTUNE & CO.** HANDMADE, GREEN, QUART, WAX SEAL. BASE READS: "FAHNSTOCK FORTUNE & CO" 40.00-50.00
FAMOUS MACHINE MADE, AQUA, 3 SIZES, GLASS LID, WIRE BAIL. *THE WIDEMOUTH FAMOUS JAR* 12.00-15.00	**FAVORITE** HANDMADE, AQUA, PINT, QUART, ZINC LID. *Favorite* 15.00-20.00	**FAXON** HANDMADE, BLUE, 3 SIZES, GLASS LID, ZINC LID. BASE READS: "FAXON-BUFFALO, NY" 6.00-8.00
FEDERAL FRUIT JAR HANDMADE, OLIVE, QUART, GLASS LID, WIRE BAIL. *FEDERAL FRUIT JAR* 75.00-100.00	**FINK & NASSE** HANDMADE, AQUA, QUART, GLASS LID, HELICAL WIRE CLOSURE. *FINK & NASSE ST LOUIS* 50.00-60.00	**F.W. FITCH CO.** CLEAR, PINT, METAL LID *The F.W. Fitch Co* 1.00-2.00
E. C. FLACCUS CO. HANDMADE, PINT, GLASS THREADED LID. (THIS JAR HAS AN ELKS HEAD & FLORAL DESIGN) VERY RARE MILK GLASS 225.00-250.00 GREEN 300.00 + AMBER 200.00-225.00 CLEAR 40.00-50.00	**E. C. FLACCUS CO.** HANDMADE, PINT, GLASS THREADED LID. (THIS JAR HAS A STEERS HEAD WITH FRUIT) MILK GLASS 225.00-250.00 GREEN 300.00 + AMBER 200.00-225.00 CLEAR 40.00-50.00	**W. & J. FLETT** HANDMADE, GREEN, QUART, GLASS LID, WIRE CLAMP. 20.00-25.00

FLICKINGER HANDMADE, AQUA, QUART, GLASS LID, WIRE BAIL JF 18.00-20.00	**THE FORSTER JAR** MACHINE MADE, CLEAR, 3 SIZES, GLASS LID, METAL SCREW BAND. THE FORSTER JAR 6.00-8.00	**FOSTER SEALFAST** MACHINE MADE, CLEAR, 3 SIZES, GLASS LID, WIRE BAIL. FOSTER SEALFAST 3.00-5.00
4 SEASONS MASON MACHINE MADE, CLEAR, 3 SIZES, ZINC LID. 4 seasons mason 2.00-4.00	**FRANK** HANDMADE, AQUA, QUART, WAX SEAL. BOTTOM READS: "WM. FRANK & SONS, PITTSBURGH." 20.00-25.00	**FRANKLIN FRUIT JAR** HANDMADE, AQUA, QUART, ZINC LID. FRANKLIN FRUIT JAR 40.00-50.00
FRANKLIN FRUIT JAR HANDMADE, AQUA, QUART, GLASS LID. FRANKLIN DEXTER FRUIT JAR 25.00-30.00	**FRIDLEY & CORNMAN'S** HANDMADE, AQUA, QUART, STOPPER TOP. FRIDLEY & CORNMAN's PATENT OCT. 25TH 1859 LADIES CHOICE 275.00-300.00	**FRUIT-KEEPER** HANDMADE, AQUA, QUART, TIN LID, CAM WIRE BAIL. FRUIT-KEEPER CO 25.00-30.00
FRUIT GROWERS HANDMADE, AQUA, 2 SIZES, WAX SEAL TRADE MARK FRUIT GROWERS Co 40.00-50.00	**THE GAYNER GLASS TOP** MACHINE MADE, CLEAR, QUART, GLASS LID, WIRE BAIL. THE GAYNER MASON 3.00-5.00	**THE GEM** HANDMADE, AQUA, QUART, WAX SEAL. THE GEM 8.00-10.00

THE GEM HANDMADE, AQUA, QUART, WAX SEAL. THE GEM 6.00-8.00	**THE GEM** HANDMADE, AQUA, 3 SIZES, GLASS LID, SCREW BAND. THE GEM 12.00-15.00	**THE GEM** HANDMADE, AQUA, 3 SIZES, GLASS LID, SCREW BAND. THE GEM 10.00-12.00
THE GEM HANDMADE, AQUA, 3 SIZES, GLASS LID, SCREW BAND. THE GEM 12.00-15.00	**THE GEM** HANDMADE, AQUA, QUART, GLASS LID, SCREW BAND. THE GEM RUTHERFORD & CO 12.00-15.00	**GEM** HANDMADE, GREEN, QUART, GLASS LID, SCREW BAND. GEM 6.00-8.00
GEM HANDMADE, GREEN, QUART, GLASS LID, METAL BAND. GEM 10.00-12.00	**GEM** HANDMADE, CLEAR, QUART, HALF GALLON, GLASS LID, ZINC BAND. Gem 4.00-6.00	**NEW GEM** MACHINE MADE, CLEAR, 3 SIZES, GLASS LID, SCREW BAND. NEW Gem 4.00-6.00
WALLACEBURG GEM MACHINE MADE, CLEAR, 3 SIZES, GLASS LID, SCREW BAND. Wallaceburg Gem 4.00-6.00	**GEM 1908** MACHINE MADE, CLEAR, 3 SIZES, GLASS LID, SCREW BAND. Gem 1908 4.00-6.00	**GENUINE MASON** HANDMADE, AQUA, 2 SIZES, ZINC LID. GENUINE MASON 6.00-8.00

GENUINE MASON MACHINE MADE, CLEAR, AQUA, 3 SIZES, ZINC LID. *Genuine Mason IPC CO* 6.00-8.00	**MASON** MACHINE MADE, AQUA, CLEAR, ZINC LID. *Genuine Mason* 6.00-8.00	**GESSNER'S** HANDMADE, CLEAR, PINT, QUART. *GESSNER'S PATENT* 150.00-175.00
GILBREDS JAR HANDMADE, AQUA, PINT, QUART, GLASS LID WITH WIRE CIRCLEING ENTIRE JAR. *GILBERDS ☆ JAR* 140.00-150.00	**GILBREDS JAR** HANDMADE, AQUA, PINT, QUART, GLASS LID WITH WIRE CIRCLEING ENTIRE JAR. *GILBERDS IMPROVED ☆* 90.00-100.00	**GJ** HANDMADE, CLEAR, 4 SIZES, ZINC LID. *GJ* 12.00-15.00
GJ CO. HANDMADE, CLEAR, 3 SIZES, ZINC LID. 20.00-25.00	**GJ MASON'S PATENT** HANDMADE, AQUA, 2 SIZES, ZINC LID. *MASON'S GJ PATENT NOV. 30TH 1858* 8.00-10.00	**GLASSBORO** HANDMADE, OLIVE, AQUA, 3 SIZES, ZINC LID. *GLASSBORO TRADE MARK* OLIVE 20.00-25.00 AQUA 12.00-15.00
GLASSBORO HANDMADE, AQUA, 3 SIZES, GLASS LID, SCREW BAND. *GLASSBORO TRADE MARK IMPROVED* 12.00-15.00	**W H GLENNY SON & CO.** AQUA, GLASS STOPPER, OT. 8 INCHES TALL. *W H GLENNY SON & Co IMPORTERS OF QUEENSWARE No.162 MAIN STREET BUFFALO N.Y.* 125.00-150.00	**GLENSHAW** MACHINE MADE, CLEAR, 3 SIZES, ZINC LID. *GLENSHAW G MASON* 3.00-5.00

GLOBE HANDMADE, CLEAR, GREEN, AMBER, 3 SIZES, GLASS LID, LEVER BAIL. GLOBE CLEAR 15.00-18.00 AMBER 30.00-35.00	**GLOCKER** MACHINE MADE, AQUA, PINT, QUART, GLASS LID, METAL CLAMP. GLOcKer TRADE MARK SANITARY PAT 1911 OTHERS PENDING 20.00-25.00	**GOLDEN STATE MASON** MACHINE MADE, CLEAR, 4 SIZES, METAL LID. GOLDEN-STATE TRADE PAT'D / S \ OTHER DEC 20 1910 PATENTS PEN. MARK MASON 12.00-15.00
GOLDEN STATE IMPROVED MACHINE MADE, CLEAR, 2 SIZES, METAL LID. IMPROVED GOLDEN-STATE PAT'D / S \ OTHER DEC 20 1910 PATS PEN MASON 12.00-15.00	**GOLDEN WEST** CLEAR, QUART, WIDE MOUTH, RING FITS. GOLDEN WEST VACUUM PACKED COFFEE CLOSSET & DEVERS PORTLAND, ORE. 1.00-3.00	**GOOD HOUSE KEEPERS** MACHINE MADE, CLEAR, 4 SIZES, ZINC LID. GOOD HOUSE KEEPERS MASON JAR 1.00-2.00
GOOD HOUSE KEEPERS MACHINE MADE, CLEAR, 4 SIZES, ZINC LID. GOOD HOUSE KEEPERS ® REGULAR MASON 1.00-2.00	**GOOD HOUSE KEEPERS** MACHINE MADE, CLEAR, 3 SIZES, ZINC LID. GOOD HOUSE KEEPERS ® WIDE MOUTH MASON 1.00-2.00	**GREEN MOUNTAIN** MACHINE MADE, GREEN, PINT, QUART, GLASS LID, WIRE BAIL. GREEN MOUNTAIN G.A.CO 12.00-15.00
GREEN MOUNTAIN MACHINE MADE, AQUA, 3 SIZES, GLASS LID, WIRE BAIL. GREEN MOUNTAIN G·A·Co. 12.00-15.00	**G S & CO.** HANDMADE, AQUA, QUART, CORKER. G.S.&CO. (ON BASE) 30.00-35.00	**H & D** HANDMADE, GREEN, QUART, WAX SEAL. BOTTOM READS: "H & D" 15.00-20.00

H & R HANDMADE, GREEN, QUART, WAX SEAL. H&R 8.00-10.00	**H & S** HANDMADE, AQUA, QUART, METAL STOPPER. H&S 350.00-400.00	**HAHNE & CO.** HANDMADE, AQUA, QUART, WAX SEAL. HAHNE ☆ 70.00-75.00
HAINES'S AQUA, 2 QT. GLASS LID. HAINES'S "IMPROVED" NE PLUS ULTRA PAT'D APRIL 21ST 1868 MCH 1ST 1870 NOV 2D 1875 175.00-200.00	**HAINE'S** HANDMADE, GREEN, QUART, GLASS LID, METAL CLAMP. HAINES 2 PATENT MARCH 1ST 1870 70.00-75.00	**HAINE'S** HANDMADE, AQUA, QUART, GLASS LID, METAL CLIP. HAINES COMBINATION 100.00-125.00
HALLE HANDMADE, GREEN, QUART, WAX SEAL. HALLE CLEVELAND O. 50.00-60.00	**HAMILTON** HANDMADE, BLUE, QUART, GLASS LID, METAL YOKE. HAMILTON 40.00-50.00	**HAMILTON** HANDMADE, CLEAR, QUART, GLASS LID, METAL CLIP. HAMILTON 40.00-50.00
HAMILTON GLASS WORKS HANDMADE, AQUA, QUART, GLASS LID, METAL YOKE, WITH SCREW. HAMILTON GLASS WORKS 175.00-200.00	**HAMILTON** HANDMADE, BLUE, QUART, GLASS LID, METAL YOKE. HAMILTON NO 9 GLASS WORKS 40.00-50.00	**HANSEE'S** HANDMADE, CLEAR, GLASS LID, WIRE LEVER. HANSEE'S HP PALACE HOME JAR 45.00-50.00

HARTELLS	HARVEST MASON	HASEROT
HANDMADE, AQUA, QUART, GLASS LID, METAL CLAMP.	MACHINE MADE, CLEAR, QUART, GLASS LID, SCREW BAND.	MACHINE MADE, AQUA, QUART, ZINC LID.
LID READS: "HARTELL'S AIRTIGHT GLASS COVER" "PATENTED OCT. 19 1858"	*Harvest* MASON	THE HASEROT COMPANY CLEVELAND MASON PATENT
50.00-60.00	6.00-8.00	12.00-15.00
HAWLEY	HAZARD	HAZEL
HANDMADE, AQUA, QUART, ZINC LID.	HANDMADE, GREEN, QUART GLASS LID, METAL CLIP.	MACHINE MADE, AQUA, PINT, QUART, GLASS LID, WIRE BAIL.
BOTTOM READS: "HAWLEY GLASS CO. HAWLEY PA."	BOTTOM READS: "HAZARD & CO. SHREWSBURY NJ"	HAZEL
12.00-15.00	10.00-12.00	12.00-15.00
HAZEL ATLAS E-Z SEAL	HAZEL ATLAS LIGHTNING	HAZEL
MACHINE MADE, CLEAR, 3 SIZES, GLASS LID, WIRE BAIL.	MACHINE MADE, CLEAR, GREEN, PINT, QUART, GLASS LID, WIRE BAIL.	MACHINE MADE, CLEAR, 2 SIZES, GLASS LID, WIRE BAIL.
HAZEL ATLAS E-Z SEAL	HAZEL ATLAS LIGHTNING SEAL	HAZEL PRESERVE JAR
8.00-10.00	8.00-10.00	6.00-8.00
HAZEL	HELME'S RAILROAD MILLS	HERO
MACHINE MADE, CLEAR, 2 SIZES, GLASS LID, WIRE BAIL.	HANDMADE, AMBER, 2 SIZES, GLASS LID, METAL BAND.	HANDMADE, GREEN, CLEAR, PINT, QUART, GLASS LID, SCREW BAND.
HAZEL [H logo] PRESERVE JAR	HELME'S RAILROAD MILLS	HERO [logo]
4.00-6.00	12.00-15.00	30.00-35.00

HERO HANDMADE, GREEN, CLEAR, QUART, GLASS LID, SCREW BAND. HERO 30.00-35.00	**HERO** HANDMADE, GREEN, PINT, QUART, GLASS LID, WIRE BAIL. HERO 30.00-35.00	**THE HERO** HANDMADE, AQUA, QUART, GLASS LID, SCREW BAND. THE HERO 30.00-35.00
THE HERO HANDMADE, AQUA, QUART, GLASS LID, SCREW BAND. THE HERO 30.00-35.00	**HERO IMPROVED** HANDMADE, AQUA, PINT, QUART, GLASS LID, SCREW BAND. HERO IMPROVED 15.00-20.00	**THE HERO IMPROVED** HANDMADE, AQUA, QUART, GLASS LID, SCREW BAND. THE HERO IMPROVED 15.00-20.00
THE HEROINE HANDMADE, AQUA, QUART, GLASS LID, SCREW BAND. THE HEROINE 25.00-30.00	**CHAS M. HIGGINS & CO.** GRAY-PINK TINT, SCREW LID. CHAS.M.HIGGINS & CO. 14 OZ BROOKLYN N.Y. 2.00-3.00	**HOLLIEANNA** MACHINE MADE, CLEAR, 3 SIZES, ZINC LID. Hollieanna MASON 4.00-6.00
HOM-PAK MACHINE MADE, CLEAR, 3 SIZES, ZINC LID. HOM-PAK MASON 2.00-3.00	**HONEST MASON** HANDMADE, AQUA, CLEAR, PINT, QUART, ZINC LID. HONEST MASON JAR PAT. 1858 12.00-15.00	**HOOSIER** HANDMADE, AQUA, QUART, THREADED GLASS LID. HOOSIER JAR 300.00-350.00

HORMEL MACHINE MADE, CLEAR, 2 SIZES, METAL LID. *(HORMEL GOOD FOOD logo)* 1.00-2.00	**THE HOWE JAR** HANDMADE, AQUA, QUART, GLASS LID, UNIQUE WIRE BAIL. *(THE HOWE JAR logo)* 40.00-50.00	**I G CO.** HANDMADE, AQUA, QUART, WAX SEAL. *(IG Co logo)* 18.00-20.00
I G A MACHINE MADE, CLEAR, QUART, METAL LID. *(IGA shield logo)* 1.00-2.00	**THE IDEAL** HANDMADE, CLEAR, AQUA, 3 SIZES, ZINC LID. *(THE IDEAL logo)* 15.00-18.00	**IDEAL WIDE MOUTH JAR** MACHINE MADE, CLEAR, 4 SIZES, ZINC LID. *(IDEAL WIDE MOUTH JAR shield logo)* 3.00-5.00
THE IMPERIAL HANDMADE, AQUA, 3 SIZES, GLASS LID, ZINC BAND. *(THE CCo IMPERIAL logo)* 15.00-20.00	**IMPROVED** HANDMADE, AQUA, QUART, GLASS LID, ZINC BAND. *(IMPROVED logo)* 12.00-15.00	**IMPROVED CROWN** MACHINE MADE, GREEN, QUART, GLASS LID, METAL BAND. *(Improved Crown script logo)* 2.00-3.00
IMPROVED CROWN HANDMADE, CLEAR, 3 SIZES, GLASS LID, ZINC LID. *(Improved Crown script logo)* 3.00-5.00	**IMPROVED GEM** QUART, GLASS LID, ZINC RING. *(Improved GEM MADE IN CANADA logo)* AMBER 45.00-50.00 OTHER 1.00-2.00	**IMPROVED GEM** HANDMADE, CLEAR, QUART PINT, GLASS LID, SCREW BAND. *(IMPROVED GEM logo)* 2.00-4.00

IMPROVED GEM MACHINE MADE, CLEAR, AQUA, 3 SIZES, GLASS LID, SCREW BAND. *Improved Gem* TRADE MARK REG'D 1.00-2.00	**IMPROVED JAM** HANDMADE, AQUA, PINT, QUART, GLASS LID, ZINC BAND. IMPROVED JAM 50.00-75.00	**IMPROVED MASON** HANDMADE, AQUA, PINT, QUART, VERY CRUDE WAX SEAL. IMPROVED MASON JAR 4.00-6.00
INDEPENDENT HANDMADE, CLEAR, AQUA, QUART, GLASS SCREW LID. INDEPENDENT 35.00-40.00	**INDEPENDENT JAR** HANDMADE, CLEAR, QUART, GLASS LID. INDEPENDENT JAR 35.00-40.00	**IVANHOE** MACHINE MADE, CLEAR, QUART, METAL LID. BOTTOM READS: "IVANHOE" 1.00-3.00
J & B FRUIT JAR HANDMADE, AQUA, PINT, QUART, ZINC LID. J&B FRUIT JAR PAT'D JUNE 14 1898 50.00-60.00	**JEANNETTE** MACHINE MADE, CLEAR, PINT, QUART, GLASS LID, SCREW BAND. Jeannette J MASON Home Packer 3.00-5.00	**JEANNETTE** MACHINE MADE, CLEAR, PINT, QUART, GLASS LID, SCREW BAND. Jeannette Home Packer 3.00-5.00
JEWELL JAR MACHINE MADE, CLEAR, 3 SIZES, GLASS LID, SCREW BAND. JEWELL JAR 6.00-8.00	**JEWELL JAR** MACHINE MADE, CLEAR, 3 SIZES, GLASS LID, SCREW BAND. JEWELL JAR MADE IN CANADA 2.00-4.00	**JOHNSON & JOHNSON** HANDMADE, COBALT BLUE, AMBER, 3 SIZES, GLASS LID, SCREW BAND. JOHNSON & JOHNSON NEW YORK AMBER 75.00-100.00

JOHNSON & JOHNSON HANDMADE, COBALT BLUE, AMBER, GLASS LID WITH CLAMP. JOHNSON & JOHNSON NEW BRUNSWICK NJ USA AMBER 15.00-18.00 COBALT BLUE 35.00-40.00	**THE KALAMAZOO** MACHINE MADE, CLEAR, PINT, QUART, ZINC LID. THE KALAMAZOO JAY B RHODES COMPANY KALAMAZOO, MICHIGAN 4.00-6.00	**KBC** MACHINE MADE, CLEAR, QUART, ZINC LID. BOTTOM READS: "KBC" 6.00-8.00
K C MASON MACHINE MADE, CLEAR, 3 SIZES, ZINC LID. KC FINEST QUALITY MASON SQUARE SPACESAVER STYLE 1.00-3.00	**K-G** MACHINE MADE, CLEAR, PINT, QUART, ZINC LID. K-G 1.00-3.00	**KEEFER'S** HANDMADE, AQUA, QUART, GLASS STOPPER, INTERNAL THREADS. KEEFFER'S NO 2 175.00-200.00
KENTUCKY HANDMADE, GREEN, QUART, WAX SEAL. KENTUCKY LG CO 50.00-60.00	**KERR ECONOMY** MACHINE MADE, CLEAR, 3 SIZES, METAL LID, CLIP. Kerr Economy TRADE MARK 2.00-4.00	**KERR ECONOMY** MACHINE MADE, CLEAR, 3 SIZES, METAL LID, CLIP. Kerr "Economy" TRADE MARK 2.00-4.00
KERR GLASS TOP MACHINE MADE, CLEAR, 4 SIZES, GLASS TOP SCREW BAND. Kerr GLASS TOP 1.00-2.00	**KERR GLASS TOP MASON** MACHINE MADE, CLEAR, 4 SIZES, GLASS LID, SCREW BAND. Kerr GLASS TOP MASON 1.00-3.00	**KERR** MACHINE MADE, CLEAR, QT. METAL LID, SCREW BAND. Kerr "SELF SEALING" TRADE MARK REG WIDE MOUTH MASON 1.00-2.00

KERR SELF SEALING MASON MACHINE MADE, CLEAR, BLUE, 3 SIZES, METAL LID, SCREW BAND. *Kerr SELF SEALING TRADE MARK REG MASON* 1.00-2.00	**KERR SELF SEALING MASON** NOTE: THERE ARE OVER 12 DIFFERENT STYLES OF THIS JAR. ALL ARE INEXPENSIVE, AND VERY COMMON. SOME ARE DATED AUG. 1st. 1915. THESE TOO ARE COMMON. THESE RANGE IN PRICE FROM 1.00-3.00. MOST OF THESE JARS ARE CLEAR, HOWEVER THERE ARE GREEN AND BLUE JARS	**KEYSTONE** MACHINE MADE, CLEAR, PINT, QUART, ZINC LID. *TRADE MARK KEYSTONE REGISTERED* 8.00-10.00
KIEFFER'S HANDMADE, GREEN, PINT, QUART, GLASS LID, METAL CLAMP. *KIEFFER'S — No. 1 —* 18.00-20.00	**THE KILNER JAR** MACHINE MADE, CLEAR, AQUA, PINT, QUART, GLASS LID, SCREW BAND. *THE KILNER JAR* 4.00-6.00	**KING** MACHINE MADE, CLEAR, 3 SIZES, GLASS LID, WIRE BAIL 12.00-15.00
KING MACHINE MADE, CLEAR, 3 SIZES, GLASS LID, WIRE BAIL *KING* 10.00-12.00	**THE KING** HANDMADE, CLEAR, AQUA, QUART, GLASS LID, IRON YOKE.. *THE KING PAT. NOV. 2. 1869* 100.00-125.00	**KINSELLA** MACHINE MADE, CLEAR, AQUA, PINT, QUART, ZINC LID. *Kinsella 1874 TRUE MASON* 6.00-8.00
KIVLAN & ONTHANK HANDMADE, LIGHT AMBER, QUART, GLASS LID, CLAMP. BOTTOM READS: "KIVLAN & ONTHANK PATD. JUNE 28 21. BOSTON" AMBER 20.00-25.00 OTHER 12.00-15.00	**KLINE** HANDMADE, BLUE, QUART, GLASS STOPPER. STOPPER READS: "A.R. KLINE PAT OCT 27 1863" 25.00-30.00	**KNIGHT PACKING CO.** MACHINE MADE, CLEAR, QUART, ZINC LID. BOTTOM READS: "KNIGHT PACKING CO." 1.00-3.00

KNOWLTON JAR HANDMADE, AQUA, CLEAR, QUART, GLASS LID, ZINC CAP. KNOWLTON VACUME ★ FRUIT JAR 18.00-20.00	**KNOX MASON** MACHINE MADE, CLEAR, 3 SIZES, ZINC LID. *Knox Mason* 3.00-5.00	**KNOX MASON** MACHINE MADE, CLEAR, 3 SIZES, METAL LID. KNOX ⟨K⟩ MASON 2.00-3.00
KOHRS MACHINE MADE, CLEAR, 4 SIZES, GLASS LID, WIRE BAIL. *Kohrs* DAVINPORT, IA. PAT'D JULY 14 1908 3.00-5.00	**K Y G W** HANDMADE, AQUA, QUART, WAX SEAL, CRUDE. KYGW 18.00-20.00	**L G CO** HANDMADE, AQUA, QUART, WAX SEAL. BASE READS: " L G CO" 18.00-20.00
L & S MACHINE MADE, CLEAR, QUART, GLASS LID, WIRE BAIL. L&S (ON BASE) 1.00-2.00	**L & W** HANDMADE, AQUA, AMBER, QUART, WAX SEAL. *L&W* AQUA 25.00-30.00	**LAFAYETTE** HANDMADE, AQUA, 3 SIZES, 3 DIFFERENT CLOSURES *Lafayette* 300.00-350.00
LAFAYETTE HANDMADE, AQUA, 3 SIZES, 3 TYPE CLOSURES. *Lafayette* 75.00-100.00	**LAM MASON** MACHINE MADE, CLEAR, QUART, ZINC LID. LAM MASON 2.00-4.00	**LAMB** MACHINE MADE, AQUA, CLEAR, 3 SIZES, ZINC LID. LAMB MASON 1.00-3.00

LAMONT GLASS CO. HANDMADE, AQUA, PINT, QUART, GLASS LID, ZINC BAND. *[GCo monogram logo]* 35.00-40.00	**THE LEADER** HANDMADE, CLEAR, AMBER, GREEN, 3 SIZES, GLASS LID, WIRE LEVER BAIL. *THE LEADER* AMBER 75.00-85.00 OTHER 30.00-35.00	**THE LEADER** HANDMADE, AQUA, AMBER, CLEAR, 3 SIZES, GLASS LID, WIRE BAIL. *THE LEADER* AMBER 75.00-85.00 OTHER 30.00-35.00
LEOTRIC HANDMADE, CLEAR, AQUA, 3 SIZES, GLASS LID, WIRE BAIL. *(LEOTRIC in oval)* 6.00-8.00	**LEOTRIC** MACHINE MADE, AQUA, CLEAR, 3 SIZES, GLASS LID, WIRE BAIL. *LEOTRIC* 8.00-10.00	**L'IDEALE** MACHINE MADE, GREEN, 4 SIZES, GLASS LID, WIRE CLIP, MODERN FRENCH JAR. *L'IDEALE* 15.00-20.00
LIGHTNING MACHINE MADE, CLEAR, 4 SIZES, GLASS LID, WIRE BAIL. *[anchor with H]* **LIGHTNING** 1.00-2.00	**LIGHTNING** HANDMADE, AQUA, AMBER, 3 SIZES, GLASS LID, WIRE BAIL. *LIGHTNING* AMBER 20.00-30.00 AQUA 4.00-6.00	**LIGHTNING** HANDMADE, AQUA, 3 SIZES, GLASS LID, WIRE BAIL. *(LIGHTNING H.W.P. in circle)* (ON BASE) 1.00-3.00
LIGHTNING HANDMADE, AQUA, AMBER, 3 SIZES, GLASS LID, WIRE BAIL. *TRADE MARK LIGHTNING* AMBER 20.00-30.00 AQUA 2.00-3.00	**LIGHTNING** MACHINE MADE, AQUA, 4 SIZES, GLASS LID, WIRE BAIL. *TRADE MARK LIGHTNING REGISTERED US PATENT OFF.* 2.00-4.00	**LINDELL GLASS CO.** HANDMADE, AMBER, QUART, WAX SEAL. BOTTOM READS:"LINDELL GLASS CO." AMBER 75.00-100.00 OTHER 20.00-25.00

LIQUID CARBONIC CO. MACHINE MADE, CLEAR, 3 SIZES, GLASS LID, WIRE BAIL. THE LIQUID *The Liquid* CARBONIC CO 1.00-2.00	**LOCKPORT MASON** MACHINE MADE, CLEAR, 3 SIZES, ZINC LID. LOCKPORT MASON 4.00-6.00	**LOCKPORT MASON IMPROVED** MACHINE MADE, AQUA, 3 SIZES, GLASS LID, SCREW BAND. LOCKPORT MASON IMPROVED 4.00-6.00
P. LORILLARD & CO. (SNUFF) HANDMADE, GREEN, AMBER, PINT, QUART, 2 QUART, GLASS LID, WIRE CLIPS. P LORILLARD & CO. 12.00-15.00	**LUSTRE** MACHINE MADE, AQUA, 3 SIZES, GLASS LID, WIRE BAIL. *Lustre* PHILADELPHIA, PA. 6.00-8.00	**LUSTRE** HANDMADE, AQUA, 3 SIZES, ZINC LID. *Lustre* 10.00-12.00
LUSTRE MACHINE MADE, AQUA, CLEAR, 3 SIZES, ZINC LID. *Lustre* R.E. TONGUE & BROS CO. PHILA 6.00-8.00	**W. W. LYMAN** HANDMADE, AQUA, QUART, THREADLESS, TAPERED METAL LID. PAT D AUG 5TH 1862 W.W. LYMAN 40.00-50.00	**LYNCHBURG** MACHINE MADE, AQUA, PINT, QUART, ZINC LID. LYNCHBURG STANDARD MASON 15.00-18.00
LYON & BOSSARD'S JAR HANDMADE, AQUA, QUART, GLASS LID, METAL YOKE. LYON & BOSSARD'S JAR EAST STROUDSBURG PA 200.00-250.00	**MACOMB** HANDMADE POTTERY, GREY, BROWN, PINT, QUART, THREADED LID. BOTTOM READS: "MACOMB, ILL." SOME DATED JAN 24 1899. 10.00-12.00	**THE MAGIC JAR** HANDMADE, AQUA, QUART, GLASS LID, METAL YOKE. MAGIC FRUIT JAR WM McCULLY CO PITTSBURGH SOLE PROPRIETORS 350.00-400.00

THE MAGIC FRUIT JAR	MALLINGER	MANSFIELD MASON
HANDMADE, AMBER, AQUA, 3 SIZES, GLASS LID, TOGGLE CLAMP.	MACHINE MADE, CLEAR, QUART, ZINC LID.	CLEAR, QUART
THE MAGIC ☆ FRUIT JAR	MALLINGER	MANSFIELD MASON
AMBER 450.00-500.00 AQUA 90.00-100.00	3.00-5.00	12.00-15.00

MANSFIELD	THE MARION JAR	MASON
MACHINE AMDE, LIGHT GREEN, 2 SIZES, GLASS LID, SCREW BAND.	HANDMADE, AQUA, 3 SIZES, ZINC LID.	MACHINE MADE, GREEN, ZINC LID.
MANSFIELD IMPROVED MASON	THE MARION JAR MASON'S PATENT NOV 30 TH 1858	MASON
12.00-15.00	10.00-12.00	2.00-4.00

THE MASON JAR

Since these jars were made in so many different sizes, styles, shapes, and colors, we are going to deviate from the pattern of this text, omitting the size. The Mason jar was made in up to 6 different sizes from the ¼ pint to the 1 gallon. The color range is from black (a molted jar with a sooty look) to clear. They have all sorts of monograms from the cross to the moon & stars. A collection of the different Masons would be an interesting and rewarding endeavor. The price of most of these Masons is still within the grasp of all collectors. Some of these jars with dominant sub-titles are found elsewhere in this book.

SOME EMBOSSINGS FOUND ON "MASON'S 1858" JARS

Port   ✠   ⌂   *Root*

Ball   ◯   Ⓒ°   *Ball*   ⌂

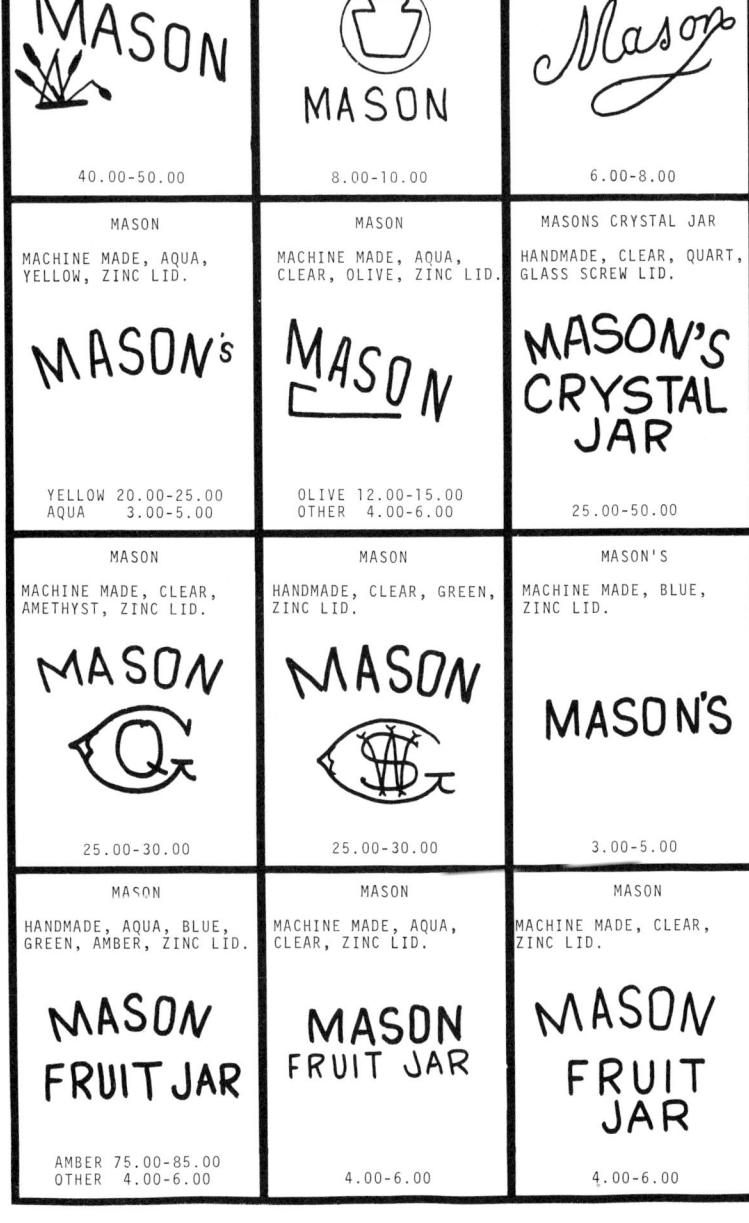

MASON HANDMADE, CLEAR, ZINC LID. *MASON JAR* 2.00-4.00	**MASON** MACHINE MADE, CLEAR, METAL LID, (MODERN) *MASON ☆ JAR* 1.00-2.00	**MASON** MACHINE MADE, AQUA, ZINC LID. *The Mason* 4.00-6.00
MASON MACHINE MADE, CLEAR, 3 SIZES, ZINC LID. *[anchor] MASON* 1.00-2.00	**MASON** HANDMADE, GREEN, GLASS LID, SCREW BAND. *MASON IMPROVED* 1.00-3.00	**MASON'S** HANDMADE, GREEN, GLASS LID, SCREW BAND. *MASON'S IMPROVED* 2.00-3.00
MASON'S HANDMADE, AQUA, GLASS LID, SCREW BAND. *TRADE MARK MASON'S IMPROVED* REVERSE → 10.00-12.00	**MASON** HANDMADE, AQUA, GLASS LID, SCREW BAND. *TRADE MARK MASON'S [CFJCo monogram] IMPROVED* 4.00-6.00	**C F J CO MASON'S IMPROVED** HANDMADE, GREEN, PINT, QUART, GLASS LID, METAL BAND. *MASON'S [CFJCo monogram] IMPROVED* 4.00-6.00
C F J CO MASONS IMPROVED HANDMADE, AQUA, QUART, GLASS LID, METAL BAND. *MASON'S IMPROVED [CFJCo monogram]* 6.00-8.00	**MASON** HANDMADE, AQUA, GLASS LID, SCREW BAND. *MASON'S IMPROVED [cross symbol]* 2.00-4.00	**MASON** HANDMADE, AQUA, GLASS LID, SCREW BAND. *[cross] MASON'S IMPROVED* 2.00-4.00

MASON HANDMADE, AQUA, GLASS LID, SCREW BAND. MASON'S IMPROVED 2 2.00-4.00	**MASON** HANDMADE, CLEAR, GLASS LID, SCREW BAND, VERY CRUDE. IMPROVED MASON JAR 4.00-6.00	**MASON'S** GREEN, QUART & 2 QUART WIDE MOUTH, GLASS LID METAL SCREW BAND. MASON'S IMPROVED BUTTER JAR 50.00-65.00
MASON HANDMADE, AMBER, AQUA, GLASS LID, SCREW BAND. THE "MASONS" IMPROVED AMBER 70.00-75.00 AQUA 20.00-25.00	**MASON'S** MACHINE MADE, CLEAR, AQUA, ZINC LID. MASON'S PATENT 1.00-3.00	**MASON'S** HANDMADE, AQUA, CLEAR, ZINC LID. MASON'S PATENT NOV 30TH 1858 6.00-8.00
MASON'S HANDMADE, AQUA, ZINC LID. MASON'S PATENT NOV 30TH 1858 10.00-12.00	**MASON'S** HANDMADE, AQUA, CLEAR, ZINC LID. MASON'S PATENT NOV. 30TH 1858 4.00-6.00	**MASON'S** HANDMADE, AMBER, GREEN, ZINC LID. MASON'S PATENT NOV 30TH 1858 AMBER Unpriced GREEN 40.00-50.00
MASON'S HANDMADE, AQUA, GREEN, ZINC LID, NOTE "BACKWARD" "N'S" MASON'S PATENT NOV 30TH 1858 10.00-12.00	**MASON'S** HANDMADE, AQUA, ZINC LID. MASON'S PATENT NOV 30TH 1858 60.00-75.00	**MASON'S** HANDMADE, AQUA, ZINC LID. MASON'S PATENT NOV 30TH 1858 6.00-8.00

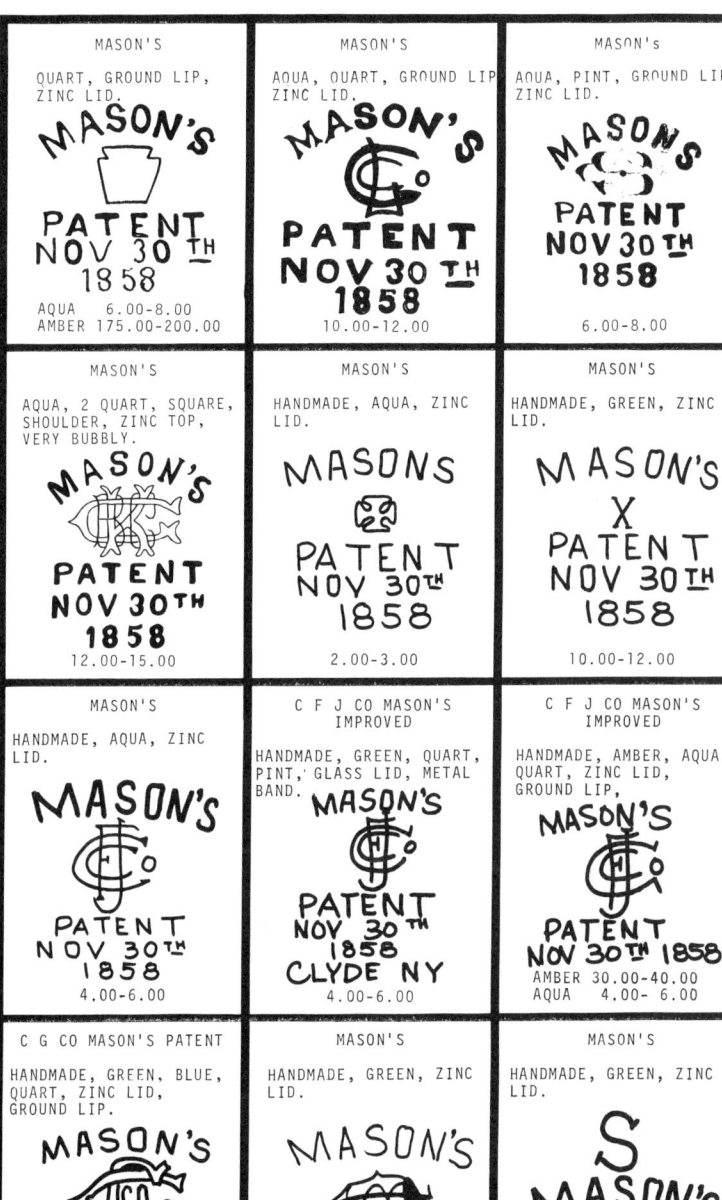

MASON'S HANDMADE, AQUA, ZINC LID. MASON'S III PATENT NOV 30TH 1858 10.00-12.00	**MASON** HANDMADE, AQUA, ZINC LID. MASON FRUIT JAR PATENT NOV 30TH 1858 10.00-12.00	**MASON'S** HANDMADE, AQUA, ZINC LID. MASON'S PATENT NOV 30TH 1858 6.00-8.00
MASON'S MACHINE MADE, AQUA, ZINC LID. MASON'S PATENT NOV 30TH 1858 3.00-5.00	**MASON'S** HANDMADE, AQUA, ZINC LID. MASON'S PATENTED JUNE 27TH 1876 75.00-90.00	**MASON** HANDMADE, AQUA, GREEN, GLASS LID, ZINC SCREW BAND. THE MASON JAR OF 1872 35.00-40.00
MASON HANDMADE, AQUA, GLASS LID, ZINC BAND. THE MASON JAR PAT. SEP. 24TH 1872 40.00-45.00	**MASON** HANDMADE, CLEAR, ZINC LID. "MASON" PATENT NOV 30 TH 1880 45.00-50.00	**MASON** HANDMADE, AQUA, ZINC LID. MASON PORCELAIN LINED 18.00-20.00
MASON HANDMADE, AQUA, ZINC LID. MASON'S UNION 140.00-150.00	**MASON** HANDMADE, AQUA, ZINC LID. Root MASON 3.00-5.00	**M C CO.** HANDMADE, AQUA, QUART, ZINC LID, WAX SEAL. BASE READS: "M C CO" 15.00-18.00

M F A MACHINE MADE, COFFEE JAR, CLEAR, QUART, ZINC LID. [MFA shield logo] 1.00-3.00	**M F G CO.** HANDMADE, AQUA, QUART, WAX SEAL. BASE READS: "M F G CO" 15.00-18.00	**M F J CO.** HANDMADE, AQUA, QUART, WAX SEAL. BASE READS: "M F J CO" 15.00-18.00
M G CO. HANDMADE, AQUA, QUART, WAX SEAL. BASE READS: "M G CO." 18.00-20.00	**MATHIAS & HENDERSON** MACHINE MADE, CLEAR, GLASS STOPPER, ENGLISH. BASE READS: "MATHIAS & HENDERSON, LIVERPOOL" 3.00-5.00	**McDONALD PERFECT SEAL** MACHINE MADE, CLEAR, 3 SIZES, GLASS LID, WIRE BAIL. McDONALD PERFECT SEAL 4.00-6.00
McDONALD NEW PERFECT SEAL MACHINE MADE, BLUE, 3 SIZES, GLASS LID, WIRE BAIL. McDONALD NEW PERFECT SEAL 4.00-6.00	**S. McKEE & CO.** HANDMADE, AQUA, QUART, WAX SEAL. S. McKEE & Co. (ON BASE) 18.00-20.00	**METRO EASY-PAK** MACHINE MADE, CLEAR, 3 SIZES, ZINC LID. METRO EASI-PAK mason 1.00-3.00
METRO EASY-PAK MACHINE MADE, CLEAR, 3 SIZES, ZINC LID. METRO EASY PAK 1.00-2.00	**MICHIGAN** MACHINE MADE, CLEAR, BLUE, 3 SIZES, ZINC LID. MICHIGAN MASON 18.00-20.00	**J. W. MIDDLEBY JR** MACHINE MADE, CLEAR, 3 SIZES, GLASS TOP, WIRE BAIL. J.W. MIDDLEBY JR 6.00-8.00

MID WEST MACHINE MADE, CLEAR, 3 SIZES, GLASS LID, SCREW BAND. Mid West CANADIAN MADE 4.00-6.00	**MILLVILLE** HANDMADE, GREEN, QUART, 2 QUART, GLASS LID, YOKE. MILLVILLE PAT. JUNE 18 1861 35.00-40.00	**MILLVILLE** HANDMADE, AMBER, AQUA, QUART, GLASS LID, YOKE. MILLVILLE ATMOSPHERIC FRUIT JAR AMBER 1000.00 + AQUA 20.00-25.00
MISSION MACHINE MADE, CLEAR, AQUA, 4 SIZES, ZINC LID. 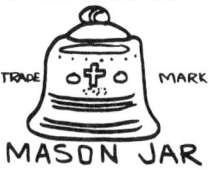 8.00-10.00	**THE MODEL JAR** HANDMADE, AQUA, QUART, OUTSIDE TAPERED LIP, PAPER CAP. THE MODEL JAR PAT<u>D</u> AUG 27. 1867. ROCHESTER N.Y. 300.00-325.00	**MODEL MASON** MACHINE MADE, AQUA, CLEAR, QUART, ZINC LID. MODEL MASON 12.00-15.00
MODEL MASON MACHINE MADE, AQUA, CLEAR, 3 SIZES, ZINC LID.  12.00-15.00	**MONARCH** MACHINE MADE, CLEAR, 3 SIZES, GLASS LID, WIRE BAIL.  6.00-8.00	**MOORE'S** HANDMADE, AQUA, QUART, GLASS STOPPER, YOKE, VERY CRUDE. Moore's PATENT DEC. 3<u>D</u> 1861 70.00-75.00
JOHN M. MOORE HANDMADE, AQUA, QUART, GLASS STOPPER, YOKE. JOHN M. MOORE MANUFACTURERS FISHERVILLE N.J. 125.00-150.00	**MORSE'S** CLEAR, QUART, GLASS TOP WIRE BAIL, SQUARE.  CHICAGO 2.00-3.00	**MOTHERS** MACHINE MADE, AQUA, 2 SIZES, ZINC LID. Mothers JAR TRADE MARK RE. TONGUE & BROS. INC. PHILA. PA. 25.00-30.00

MOUNTAIN MASON MACHINE MADE, CLEAR, 3 SIZES, ZINC LID. Mountain Mason 12.00-15.00	**MY CHOICE** HANDMADE, AQUA, HALF GALLON, GLASS LID, CLAMP. My Choice LID & BOTTOM READ: "PAT. JAN. 3RD. 1888" 175.00-200.00	**MYERS TEST JAR** HANDMADE, GREEN, QUART, GLASS LID. YOKE Myers Test Jar 75.00-100.00
NATIONAL HANDMADE, AQUA, QUART, METAL LID. National PATENTED JUNE 27 1876 150.00-175.00	**NATIONAL PRESERVE CAN** HANDMADE, AQUA, QUART, GLASS LID, CLAMP.  250.00-300.00	**NATIONAL** CLEAR, HALF-GALLON, ZINC LID. National SUPER MASON 8.00-10.00
NEW MASON VACUUM AQUA, QUART, GLASS LID WIRE CLAMP. NEW MASON VACUUM FRUIT JAR KNOWLTON PATENT JUNE 9TH 1908 40.00-50.00	**NEWMAN'S** HANDMADE, AQUA, QUART, CLOSURE UNKNOWN. NEWMAN'S PATENT DEC. 20TH 1859 300.00-350.00	**NEWMAN'S** HANDMADE, AQUA, QUART, METAL THREADLESS LID. NEWMAN'S PATENT DEC. 20TH 1859 300.00-350.00
NEWMARK MACHINE MADE, CLEAR, QUART, ZINC LID. Newmark Special Extra 8.00-10.00	**NEWMARK** MACHINE MADE, CLEAR, 3 SIZES, ZINC LID. Newmark Special Extra MASON JAR 8.00-10.00	**THE NIFTY** HANDMADE, CLEAR, QUART, GLASS LID, CLIP. The Nifty 25.00-30.00

NONPAREIL HANDMADE, AQUA, QUART, TIN LID. NONPAREIL PATENTED JULY 17 1866 200.00-250.00	**NORGE** MACHINE MADE, CLEAR, QUART, GLASS LID, METAL BAND. *Norge* 8.00-10.00	**OHIO QUALITY MASON** MACHINE MADE, CLEAR, 3 SIZES, ZINC LID. OHIO QUALITY MASON 10.00-12.00
OHIO HANDMADE, CLEAR, 3 SIZES, ZINC LID. OHIO QUALITY MASON 10.00-12.00	**THE OHIO** HANDMADE, AQUA, QUART, 2 QUART, GLASS LID, WIRE CLIP THE OHIO NO. 2 1876 MADE BY THE OHIO FRUIT JAR CO. OF UPPER SANDUSKY, O. 350.00-400.00	**OLD JUDGE** CLEAR, TAPERED, 1/4 PT. METAL LID. OLD JUDGE QUALITY PRODUCTS 1.00-2.00
OPLER BROTHERS MACHINE MADE, CLEAR, QUART, GLASS LID, WIRE BAIL. OPLER BROTHERS INC. COCOA AND CHOCOLATE 4.00-6.00	**N. OSBURN** HANDMADE, DARK AQUA, QUART, WAX SEAL. N. OSBURN. ROCHESTER N.Y. 225.00-250.00	**OSOTITE** HANDMADE, AQUA, 2 SIZES, GLASS LID CLIP. OSOTITE 8.00-10.00
PCG CO HANDMADE, AQUA, QUART WAX SEAL. BOTTOM READS: "P C G CO." 15.00-18.00	**PACIFIC GLASS WORKS** HANDMADE, AQUA, QUART, GLASS LID, SCREW BAND. PACIFIC S.F. GLASS WORKS 25.00-30.00	**PACIFIC MASON** MACHINE MASON, CLEAR, 3 SIZES, ZINC LID. *Pacific* MASON 8.00-10.00

NEW PARAGON HANDMADE, AQUA, QUART, GLASS LID, CLAMPS. NEW PARAGON 90.00-100.00	**PANSY** **20 PANELS** HANDMADE, AQUA, QUART, VERY RARE. PANSY 125.00-150.00	**PATENT SEPT. 18 1860** HANDMADE, AQUA, QUART, WAX SEAL, VERY CRUDE. PATENT SEPT 18 1860 75.00-80.00
PATENTED JUNE 27 1865 HANDMADE, AQUA, QUART, GLASS LID, METAL CLAMP. PATENTED JUNE 27 1865 200.00-250.00	**THE PEARL** HANDMADE, AQUA, QUART, GLASS LID, ZINC BAND. THE PEARL 25.00-30.00	**THE PEARL** HANDMADE, AQUA, QUART, GLASS LID, SCREW BAND. THE PEARL 25.00-30.00
PEERLESS HANDMADE, AQUA, 3 SIZES, GLASS LID, YOKE PEERLESS 85.00-100.00	**THE PENN** HANDMADE, GREEN QUART, WAX SEALER, FOOTED BASE. THE PENN 125.00-150.00	**PEORIA POTTERY** WHEEL MADE, POTTERY JAR PINT, QUART, GREY, BROWN, GROVE RING WAX SEAL. BASE READS: "PEORIA INSPECTED POTTERY" 15.00-18.00
PERFECTION HANDMADE, CLEAR, PINT, QUART, GLASS LID, UNIQUE WIRE BAIL. PERFECTION 30.00-40.00	**PERFECT SEAL** CLEAR, QUART, SQUARE, GLASS LID, WIRE BAIL. The PERFECT SEAL WIDE MOUTH 4.00-6.00	**PERFECT SEAL** AMBER, SQUARE, QUART, WIRE BAIL. The PERFECT SEAL ADJUSTABLE 18.00-20.00

PORCELAIN LINED HANDMADE, AQUA, QUART, GLASS LID, ZINC BAND. *PORCELAIN LINED* 15.00-20.00	**POTTER & BODINE** HANDMADE, AQUA, QUART, GLASS LID, YOKE. *Potter & Bodine Philadelphia* 85.00-95.00	**POTTER & BODINES** HANDMADE, AQUA, QUART, WAX SEAL. POTTER & BODINES AIRTIGHT FRUIT JAR PHILADA 375.00-400.00
PREMIUM MACHINE MADE, CLEAR, 3 SIZES, GLASS LID, SPRING CLIP. *PREMIUM* COFFEYVILLE, KAS 15.00-20.00	**PREMIUM** MACHINE MADE, CLEAR, 2 SIZES, GLASS LID, SPRING CLIP. *PREMIUM* 15.00-20.00	**PREMIUM** MACHINE MADE, CLEAR, 3 SIZES, GLASS LID, SPRING CLIP. *Premium* IMPROVED 15.00-20.00
PRESTO MACHINE MADE, CLEAR, 3 SIZES, ZINC LID. *Presto* 1.00-2.00	**PRESTO GLASS TOP** MACHINE MADE, CLEAR, 3 SIZES, GLASS LID, WIRE BAIL *Presto* GLASS TOP 1.00-2.00	**PRESTO SUPREME MASON** MACHINE MADE, CLEAR, 4 SIZES, ZINC LID. *Presto* SUPREME MASON 1.00-2.00
PRESTO WIDE MOUTH MACHINE MADE, CLEAR, 4 SIZES, GLASS LID, WIRE BAIL. *Presto* WIDE MOUTH 1.00-2.00	**PRINCESS** MACHINE MADE, AQUA, 3 SIZES, GLASS LID, WIRE BAIL. *PRINCESS* 12.00-15.00	**PRINCESS** MACHINE MADE, CLEAR, 3 SIZES, GLASS LID, WIRE BAIL. PRINCESS 15.00-18.00

PROTECTOR HANDMADE, AQUA, QUART, METAL LID, WIRE CLIP. PROTECTOR 35.00-40.00	**PROTECTOR** HANDMADE, AQUA, QUART, 6 SIDED, METAL LID, WIRE CLIP. PROTECTOR 35.00-45.00	**THE PURITAN** HANDMADE, AQUA, QUART, GLASS LID, CLAMP. THE PURITAN 150.00-175.00
PUTNAM GLASS WORKS HANDMADE, AQUA, QUART, WAX SEAL. BASE READS: "PUTNAM GLASS WORKS, ZANESVILLE O" 20.00-25.00	**Q G** MACHINE MADE, CLEAR, 3 SIZES, ZINC LID. QG 25.00-30.00	**QUART STANDARD** HANDMADE AQUA, QUART, WAX SEAL. QUART STANDARD 18.00-20.00
QUEEN MACHINE MADE, CLEAR, 3 SIZES, GLASS LID, WIRE BAIL. K S Co Queen WIDE MOUTH ADJUSTABLE 2.00-4.00	**QUEEN** MACHINE MADE, CLEAR, 3 SIZES, GLASS LID, WIRE BAIL. K S Co Queen WIDE MOUTH ADJUSTABLE 2.00-3.00	**THE QUEEN** HANDMADE, AQUA, PINT, QUART, GLASS LID, IRON YOKE WITH SCREW. PAT^D DEC. 28th 1958 THE QUEEN PAT^D JUNE 16TH 1868 40.00-50.00
THE QUEEN HANDMADE, AQUA, PINT, QUART, GLASS LID, ZINC BAND. THE QUEEN 25.00-30.00	**THE QUEEN** HANDMADE, AQUA, PINT, QUART, GLASS LID, SCREW BAND. THE QUEEN 15.00-18.00	**THE QUEEN** HANDMADE, AQUA, QUART, CRUDE WAX SEAL. THE QUEEN 50.00-60.00

THE QUEEN HANDMADE, AQUA, 3 SIZES, GLASS LID, SCREW BAND. PATD DEC 28TH 1858 THE QUEEN PATD JUNE 16TH 1868 30.00-35.00	**QUICK SEAL** MACHINE MADE, CLEAR, 3 SIZES, GLASS LID, WIRE BAIL. *Quick Seal* 2.00-4.00	**QUICK SEAL** MACHINE MADE, AQUA, CLEAR, 3 SIZES, GLASS LID, WIRE BAIL *Quick Seal* PAT'D JULY 14 1908 2.00-4.00
QUONG HOP & CO. MACHINE MADE, CLEAR, PINT, QUART, GLASS LID, WIRE BAIL. 12 OZ NET [Chinese characters] QUONG HOP & CO. 133 WAVERLY PLACE S.F. CALIF. 3.00-5.00	**RAG** (RUTH A. GILCHRIST) 25.00-30.00	**RAU'S** HANDMADE, AQUA, CLEAR, PINT, QUART, WAX SEAL. RAU'S IMPROVED GROVE RING JAR 25.00-30.00
RED MASON HANDMADE, AQUA, CLEAR, 3 SIZES, ZINC LID. RED- MASON'S PATENT NOV 30TH 1858 8.00-10.00	**RED MASON** HANDMADE, AQUA, 3 SIZES ZINC LID. RED- MASON 6.00-8.00	**REED'S** MACHINE MADE, CLEAR, QUART, 2 QUART, GLASS LID, WIRE CLAMP. *Reeds* Eugene O. Reed CHICAGO 3.00-5.00
REGAL HANDMADE, CLEAR, QUART, GLASS LID, REGAL 2.00-4.00	**REID** HANDMADE, AQUA, QUART, GLASS CONE SHAPED LIP WITH TWO POURING LIPS. REID 250.00-300.00	**REID, MURDOCK CO.** MACHINE MADE, CLEAR, QUART, ZINC LID. REID MURDOCK CO CHICAGO 2.00-3.00

RELIABLE MACHINE MADE, CLEAR, 3 SIZES, METAL LID. *Reliable* HOME CANNING MASON 2.00-3.00	**RELIANCE** MACHINE MADE, CLEAR, 3 SIZES, ZINC LID. RELIANCE BRAND WIDE MOUTH MASON 2.00-3.00	**RHODES** MACHINE MADE, AQUA, 3 SIZES, ZINC LID. FILL TO THIS LINE ONE FULL LIQUID QT. *Jay B Rhodes* KALAMAZOO MICH. 4.00-6.00
3 RIVERS MACHINE MADE, CLEAR, PINT, QUART, ZINC LID. BOTTOM READS: "3 RIVERS" 1.00-2.00	**ROGERS** MACHINE MADE, CLEAR, AMETHYST, GLASS TOP, WIRE BAIL, SQUARE. ROGERS THE B.C. SUGAR TRADE MARK REG'D REFINING CO. GOLDEN SYRUP VANCOUVER, B.C. PERFECT SEAL JAR 20.00-25.00	**ROOT** HANDMADE, AQUA, GREEN, YELLOW, PINT, QUART, ZINC LID. *Root* 5.00-7.00
THE ROSE MACHINE MADE, CLEAR, QUART, GLASS LID, SCREW BAND. *The Rose* 35.00-40.00	**THE ROSE** MACHINE MADE, CLEAR, 3 SIZES, ZINC LID. *The Rose* IMPERIAL 12.00-15.00	**ROYAL** HANDMADE, AQUA, QUART, GLASS LID, ZINC BAND. ROYAL 50.00-75.00
ROYAL HANDMADE, AQUA, QUART, GLASS LID, SCREW BAND. ROYAL OF 1876 75.00-100.00	**ROYAL** MACHINE MADE, AMBER, CLEAR, GREEN, GLASS LID, WIRE BAIL. ROYAL TRADE MARK AMBER 45.00-50.00 OTHER 6.00-8.00	**ROYAL** AQUA, CLEAR, GLASS LID, WIRE BAIL. ROYAL 884 TRADE MARK FULL MEASURE REGISTERED PINT 8.00-10.00

SAFE HANDMADE, CLEAR, 2 SIZES, TIN DISC, SPRING CLIP. SAFE 8.00-10.00	**SAFETY** HANDMADE, AMBER, AQUA, QUART, GLASS LID, CLIP. SAFETY AMBER 75.00-85.00 AQUA 35.00-40.00	**SAFETY SEAL** MACHINE MADE, CLEAR, AQUA, PINT, QUART, GLASS LID, WIRE BAIL. SAFETY SEAL MADE IN CANADA 3.00-5.00
SAFE SEAL MACHINE MADE, CLEAR, 3 SIZES, GLASS LID, WIRE BAIL. SAFE SEAL 4.00-6.00	**SAFE SEAL** MACHINE MADE, CLEAR, AQUA, 3 SIZES, GLASS LID, WIRE BAIL. SAFE SEAL PAT'D JULY 14 1908 4.00-6.00	**SAFETY VALVE** HANDMADE, AQUA, QUART, 2 QUART, GLASS LID, YOKE. SAFETY VALVE PAT'D MAY 21 1895 8.00-10.00
SAFETY MACHINE MADE, AQUA, 3 SIZES, GLASS LID, SCREW BAND. SAFETY WIDE MOUTH MASON 10.00-12.00	**SAMCO** MACHINE MADE, CLEAR, 4 SIZES, ZINC LID. Samco Genuine MASON 1.00-2.00	**SAMCO** MACHINE MADE, CLEAR, 3 SIZES, ZINC LID. Samco SUPER MASON 1.00-2.00
SAMCO CLEAR, QUART, ZINC LID. Samco SUPER JAR 1.00-2.00	**SANETY** HANDMADE, AQUA, QUART, ZINC LID. SANETY WIDE MOUTH MASON SALEM GLASS WORKS SALEM, N.J. 12.00-15.00	**SANFORD** HANDMADE, AQUA, QUART, ZINC LID. SANFORD 327 5.00-7.00

SANITAS MACHINE MADE, AQUA, PINT, QUART, ZINC LID. SANITAS NUT FOOD CO. LTD BATTLE CREEK, MICH USA. 2.00-4.00	**SCHRAM** MACHINE MADE, AQUA, 3 SIZES, METAL CAP. *Schram Automatic Sealer* 8.00-10.00	**SCHRAM** MACHINE MADE, CLEAR, 4 SIZES, METAL CAP, CLIP. *Schram AUTOMATIC SEALER* 6.00-8.00
THE SCRANTON JAR HANDMADE, AQUA, QUART, GLASS LID, UNIQUE LATCH. THE SCRANTON JAR 250.00-300.00	**SEALFAST** MACHINE MADE, CLEAR, AQUA, 4 SIZES, GLASS LID, WIRE BAIL. SEALFAST BOTTOM READS "FOSTER" 1.00-3.00	**SEALTITE** HANDMADE, CLEAR, 3 SIZES, GLASS LID, WIRE BAIL. SEALTITE 8.00-10.00
SEALTITE GREEN, QUART, MACHINE MADE, METAL SCREW TOP. SEALTITE WIDE MOUTH MASON 8.00-10.00	**SEALTITE** HANDMADE, AQUA, 2 SIZES, GLASS LID, CLEAR WIRE BAIL. *Seal Tite* 8.00-10.00	**SECURITY** HANDMADE, CLEAR, QUART, GLASS LID, WIRE BAIL. *Security* 8.00-10.00
SECURITY SEAL HANDMADE, CLEAR, 3 SIZES, GLASS LID, WIRE BAIL. SECURITY SEAL 4.00-6.00	**SELCO** MACHINE MADE, CLEAR, BLUE, 3 SIZES, GLASS LID, WIRE BAIL. SELCO SURETY SEAL 3.00-5.00	**SELCO** MACHINE MADE, CLEAR, BLUE, 3 SIZES, GLASS LID, WIRE BAIL. SELCO SURETY SEAL PAT'D JULY 14 1908 3.00-5.00

SELF SEALING MACHINE MADE, CLEAR, AQUA, 3 SIZES, GLASS LID. "SELF SEALING" TRADE MARK REG 3.00-5.00	**SIERRA** MACHINE MADE, CLEAR, 3 SIZES, ZINC LID. *Sierra* **MASON JAR** MADE IN CALIFORNIA 10.00-12.00	**SILICON** MACHINE MADE, AQUA, BLUE, 3 SIZES, GLASS LID, WIRE BAIL. SILICON GLASS COMPANY PITTSBURGH PENNA. 12.00-15.00
THE SMALLEY MACHINE MADE, CLEAR, 3 SIZES, GLASS LID, WIRE BAIL. TRADE MARK THE SMALLEY SELF SEALER 6.00-8.00	**THE SMALLEY** MACHINE MADE, CLEAR, 3 SIZES, GLASS LID, WIRE BAIL. THE SMALLEY SELF SEALER WIDE MOUTH 6.00-8.00	**THE SMALLEY** MACHINE MADE CLEAR, 3 SIZES, GLASS LID, WIRE BAIL. TRADE MARK "THE SMALLEY" SELF SEALER 6.00-8.00
SMALLEY'S NU-SEAL MACHINE MADE, CLEAR, 3 SIZES, GLASS LID, WIRE BAIL. SMALLEY'S NU-SEAL TRADE MARK 8.00-10.00	**SMALLEY'S** CLEAR, PINT & 1/2 PT. GLASS LID, WIRE BAIL. SMALLEY'S ROYAL TRADE MARK NU-SEAL 10.00-15.00	**J. P. SMITH & SON** HANDMADE, AQUA, QUART, WAX SEAL. JP SMITH SON & CO. PITTSBURGH 30.00-35.00
T. A. SNIDER MACHINE MADE, AQUA, 2 SIZES, ZINK LID. *The TA Snider Preserve Co Cincinnati O* 10.00-12.00	**SOCIETE** MACHINE MADE, CLEAR, AQUA, 3 SIZES, GLASS LID, WIRE BAIL. *Societé* 2.00-4.00	**SOUTHERN** MACHINE MADE, CLEAR, 3 SIZES, ZINC LID. *Southern* DOUBLE SEAL **MASON** 12.00-15.00

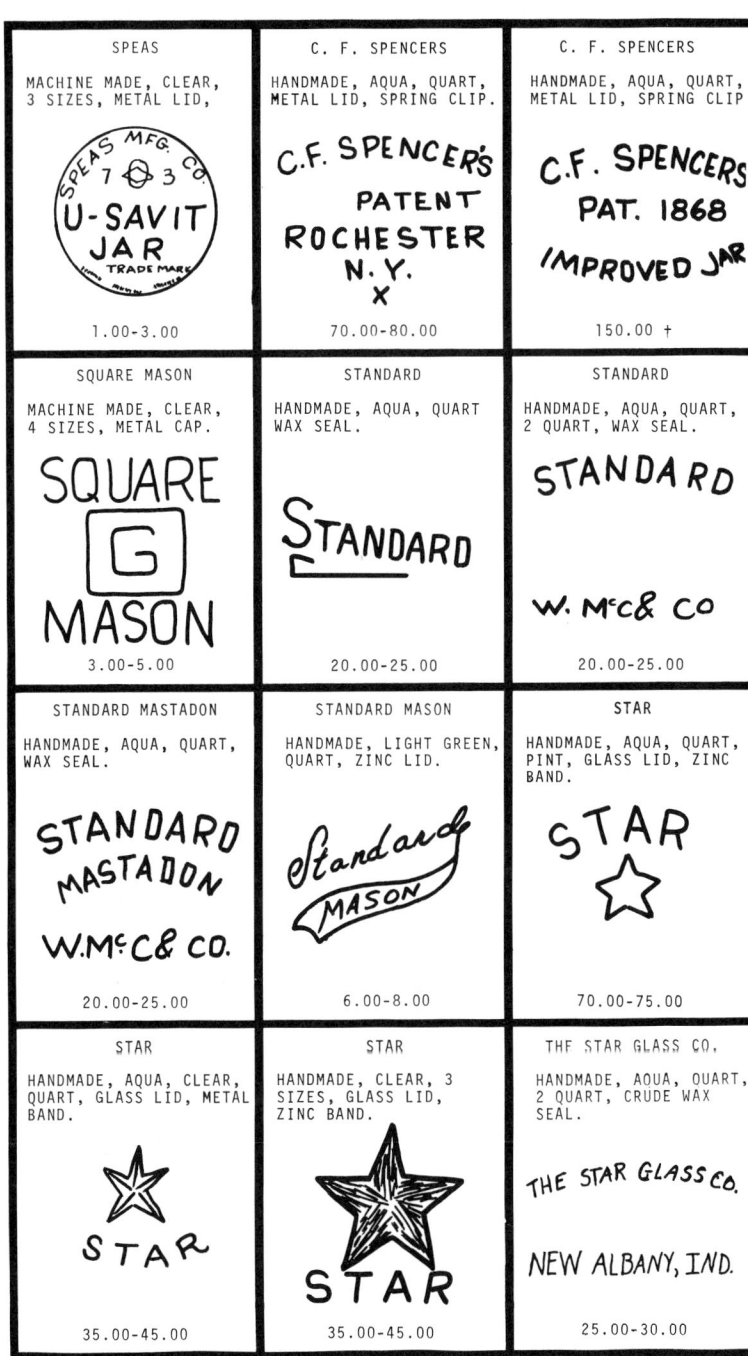

STAR & CRESCENT HANDMADE, AQUA, QUART, GLASS DISC, ZINC LID. STAR & CRESCENT PAT. MAR. 11TH 1890 75.00-100.00	**STERLING MASON** MACHINE MADE, CLEAR, 3 SIZES, ZINC LID. Sterling MASON 1.00-2.00	**STEVEN'S** HANDMADE, GREEN, QUART, 2 QUART, WAX SEAL. STEVEN'S PATD JULY 27 1875 40.00-50.00
STEVENS HANDMADE, AQUA, QUART, HALF GALLON, WAX SEAL. STEVENS TIN TOP PAT.D. JULY, 27, 1875 75.00-85.00	**STONE** POTTERY TYPE, GREY, QUART, ZINC LID. STONE MASON FRUIT JAR UNION STONEWARE REDWING MINN. 15.00-18.00	**A. STONE & CO.** HANDMADE, AQUA, QUART, INTERNAL SCREW THREADS. A STONE & CO. PHILADA 300.00 +
SUN HANDMADE, GREEN, QUART, GLASS LID, CLAMP. SUN TRADE MARK 50.00-55.00	**SURE** HANDMADE, AQUA, QUART, GLASS LID, SPRING WIRE CLIP. SURE 200.00 +	**SURE SEAL** MACHINE MADE, AQUA, 3 SIZES, GLASS LID, WIRE BAIL.  SURE SEAL MADE FOR L. BAMBERGER & CO. 10.00-12.00
SURE SEAL MACHINE MADE, AQUA, CLEAR, 3 SIZES, GLASS LID, WIRE BAIL.  Sure Seal 4.00-6.00	**SWAYZEE'S** MACHINE MADE, AQUA, PINT, QUART, ZINC LID. SWAYZEE'S IMPROVED MASON 3.00-5.00	**SWAYZEE'S** MACHINE MADE, AQUA, 3 SIZES, ZINC LID. SWAYZEE'S IMPROVED MASON 4.00-6.00

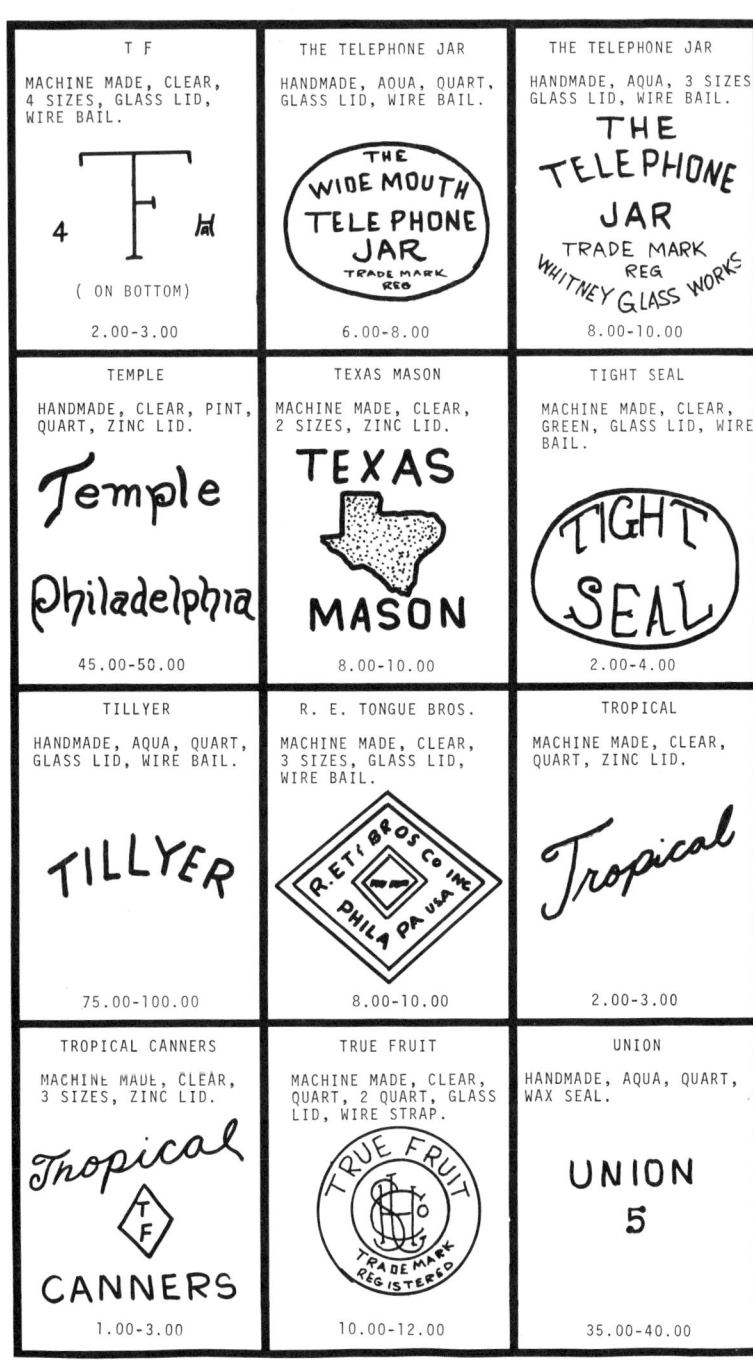

UNITED DRUG CO. MACHINE MADE, CLEAR, 3 SIZES, GLASS LID, SIDE CLAMPS. UNITED DRUG CO. 8.00-10.00	**UNIVERSAL** MACHINE MADE, CLEAR, QUART, ZINC LID. UNIVERSAL 3.00-5.00	**UNIVERSAL** AQUA, QUART, ZINC LID, (UPSIDE DOWN) L.F.&Co. UNIVERSAL (upside down) 4.00-6.00
VACUUM MACHINE MADE, CLEAR, PINT, GLASS LID. Vacuum 10.00-15.00	**THE VACUUM SEAL** HANDMADE, CLEAR, QUART, TAPERED NECK, PAPER DISC. THE VACUUM SEAL FRUIT JAR PATENTED NOV. 1ST 1904 DETROIT 50.00-75.00	**THE VALVE JAR** HANDMADE, GREEN, QUART, GLASS LID, UNIQUE WIRE CLAMP. RARE. THE VALVE JAR CO PHILADELPHIA PATENT MARCH 10 1868 125.00-150.00
THE VAN VLIET HANDMADE, AQUA, 3 SIZES, GLASS LID, WIRE ENCIRCLES ENTIRE JAR. THE VAN VLIET JAR OF 1881 225.00-250.00	**VETERAN** MACHINE MADE, CLEAR, 2 SIZES, GLASS LID, WIRE BAIL. VETERAN 15.00-20.00	**VICTOR** AQUA, QUART, GLASS LID, METAL CLAMP. THE VICTOR PATENTED 1899 30.00-40.00
VICTORY MACHINE MADE, CLEAR, 3 SIZES, WIRE CLAMP. Victory HOM-PAK MASON 1.00-3.00	**VICTORY** MACHINE MADE, CLEAR, 3 SIZES, GLASS LID, WIRE CLAMP. TOP READS: "VICTORY REG'D 1925" 4.00-6.00	**VICTORY** HANDMADE, AQUA, 3 SIZES, GLASS LID, ZINC BAND. PAT'D FEBY 9TH 1864 VICTORY REISD JUNE 22° 1867 30.00-35.00

W	W & CO.	WALES
HANDMADE, AQUA, 2 SIZES, WAX SEAL.	HANDMADE, AQUA, QUART, 2 QUART, WAX SEAL.	HANDMADE, AQUA, QUART, GLASS LID, METAL CLIP.
W	BOTTOM READS: W & CO.	BOTTOM READS: "GEO. E. WALES. NEWTON CENTER, MASS. PAT. JULY 11 1893"
3.00-5.00	25.00-30.00	15.00-18.00
WAN-ETA	WEARS	WEARS
MACHINE MADE, CLEAR, AMBER, GREEN, PINT, ZINC LID.	MACHINE MADE, AQUA, CLEAR, 3 SIZES, GLASS LID, WIRE BAIL.	MACHINE MADE, AQUA, CLEAR, 3 SIZES, GLASS LID, WIRE BAIL.
WAN-ETA COCOA BOSTON	THE WEARS JAR	WEARS
4.00-8.00	10.00-12.00	12.00-15.00
WEIR	WHITE CROWN MASON	WEIDEMAN
POTTERY JAR WITH GLASS LID & WIRE BAIL. (CAM LEVER)	MACHINE MADE, AQUA, 3 SIZES, ZINC LID.	MACHINE MADE, 3 SIZES CLEAR GLASS LID, WIRE BAIL.
AMBER LID READS: "THE WEIR PATENTED MARCH 1ST. 1892"	WHITE CROWN MASON	WEIDMAN BOY BRAND CLEVELAND
8.00-10.00	8.00-10.00	4.00-6.00
WHITNEY MASON	WHITNEY MASON	D. D. WILCOX
HANDMADE, AQUA, 3 SIZES, ZINC LID.	HANDMADE, AQUA, 3 SIZES, ZINC LID.	HANDMADE, AQUA, 3 SIZES, GLASS LID, WIRE BAIL.
WHITNEY MASON PAT'D 1858	WHITNEY MASON PAT'D 1858	PAT$^\underline{D}$ MARCH 26 1867 B.B WILCOX 8
18.00-20.00	6.00-8.00	50.00-60.00

THE WINSLOW HANDMADE, AQUA, QUART, GLASS LID, IRON YOKE, THUMB SCREW. THE WINSLOW IMPROVED VALVE JAR 175.00-200.00	**WINSLOW JAR** HANDMADE, AQUA, QUART, GLASS LID, WIRE CLIP. WINSLOW JAR 45.00-50.00	**WOODBURY** HANDMADE, AQUA, 3 SIZES, GLASS LID, METAL CLIP. WOODBURY 20.00-25.00
WOODBURY HANDMADE, AQUA, 3 SIZES, GLASS LID, METAL CLIP. WOODBURY (with monogram) 20.00-25.00	**WOODBURY** HANDMADE, AQUA, 3 SIZES, GLASS LID, METAL CLIP. WOODBURY IMPROVED 20.00-25.00	**WORCESTER** HANDMADE, AQUA, QUART, TAPERED STOPPER, UNKNOWN WORCESTER 85.00-100.00
A.W.L. WRIGHT HANDMADE, AQUA, QUART, WAX SEAL. A.W.L. WRIGHT 25.00-30.00	**YEOMAN'S** HANDMADE, AQUA, QUART, HALF GALLON, CORK STOPPER. YEOMAN'S FRUIT BOTTLE 40.00-50.00	**CLOSURES** THERE IS A MARKET FOR ODD TOPS & CLOSURES. THE PRICE RANGES FROM $2.00-35.00 EACH. COMMON GLASS LIDS & ZINC LIDS USUALLY SELL FOR 10¢ TO 25¢ EACH. DEALERS WILL USUALLY PAY 5¢ - 10¢ EACH IN QUANITY.
UNMARKED JARS GLASS LID WIRE BAIL $1. WAX SEAL 5.00-10.00 CORKERS 12.00-15.00 MIDGETS 5.00- 8.00 HALF PINTS 3.00-5.00 AMBERS 8.00-10.00 STONE JARS 4.00-8.00 WHITTLED 3.00-5.00 APPLE GREEN 5.00-8.00 HONEY BROWN 8.00-10.00 COBALT 25.00-40.00